D1151646

LEARNING TO RIDE A MOTORCYCLE

Údarás Um Shábháilteacht Ar Bhóithre
Road Safety Authority

First published by Údarás Um Shábháilteacht Ar Bhóithre / Road Safety Authority 2012

© 2012 Údarás Um Shábháilteacht Ar Bhóithre / Road Safety Authority

ISBN 978-0-9567931-1-9

10 9 8 7 6 5 4 3 2 1

Údarás Um Shábháilteacht Ar Bhóithre
Road Safety Authority

Páirc Ghnó Ghleann na Muaidhe, Cnoc an tSabhaircín,
Bóthar Bhaile Átha Cliath, Béal an Átha, Co. Mhaigh Eo.

Moy Valley Business Park, Primrose Hill, Dublin Road,
Ballina, Co. Mayo.

locall: 1890 50 60 80   fax: (096) 25 252
email: info@rsa.ie   website: www.rsa.ie

Every effort has been made to ensure the accuracy and reliability of information contained
in this book. The Road Safety Authority cannot accept responsibility for any inaccuracies or
errors, and any reliance that readers place in this book or in the information contained in it
is at their own risk. Information in this book is for guidance only.

In no event will the Road Safety Authority be liable for any loss or damage, including
without limitation, indirect or consequential loss or damage, or any loss or damage
whatsoever arising out of, or in connection with the use of this book.

Foreword

Building a strong safety culture on Irish roads is the core mission of the RSA, one that is centred very firmly on the behaviour of all road users.

In the case of motorcyclists, research from all around the world tells us that the manner in which people learn to ride is a key factor in their future behaviour on the road, and they are more likely to be safe and competent motorcyclists when they have learned within a staged and formal process, and where they have taken responsibility for their own learning experience.

The purpose of this book is to help learner motorcyclists to do just that and to work with an Approved Driving Instructor (ADI) to step through the various stages in learning how to ride. The first step is to take a course of Initial Basic Training in which you will learn the basic skills. After that you will need to practise -- with the help of your ADI and on your own.

Learning to ride a motorcycle will give you a great sense of independence, but with that independence comes responsibility for your own safety and that of other road users. Every time you sit on a motorcycle, you are accepting that responsibility.

Encouraging learner motorcyclists to take responsibility for their own learning is at the heart of this book. Learners are asked to make commitments about what they have learnt and about their own future behaviour. Your ADI will help you to acquire the skills and knowledge you need to make each of these commitments.

We are confident that this book can make a contribution to continuing the improvement in Irish road safety. We wish all learner motorcyclists many years of safe riding.

Noel Brett, Chief Executive Officer, RSA

Contents

Using this book

You've made the big step of deciding that you want to learn how to ride a motorcycle. You've been looking forward to learning to ride a motorcycle for quite some time now, you're eager to get started, and you're probably also a little nervous.

To become a safe and competent motorcyclist, you need:

- To learn – about the rules of the road, about your motorcycle, and about the law;
- To take a course of Initial Basic Training (IBT) with an IBT-registered Approved Driving Instructor (ADI);
- To plan a programme of learning; and
- To practise, practise, practise.

Road safety organisations around the world have tried to find out what makes people good and safe road users (both of motorcycles and of cars). One thing they found is that the way people learn how to ride or drive is extremely important. In particular, one thing was clear – that learners become better and safer road users when they have gone through a structured and planned learning programme.

The purpose of this book is to help you to take responsibility for your own learning, to organise a course of Initial Basic Training, to plan your own programme of learning, and to develop your motorcycling skills safely and efficiently. You won't learn how to ride by just reading about it – but if you plan how you learn, the chances are you'll come to be a safe, competent and responsible motorcyclist.

Chapter by chapter

This book lays out a typical path that you might follow as a learner driver.

Chapter 1, Getting yourself organised: this chapter deals with how you (as the learner) can take responsibility and plan for your own learning. You need to enrol on a course of Initial Basic Training, and you need to know the legal and safety requirements that you must follow as a motorcyclist.

Chapter 2, Getting started: this chapter covers many of the things you need to know before you begin to ride. Once you have chosen a motorcycle that is suited to your needs, and you have kitted yourself out with the correct safety equipment and protective clothing, you're ready to learn (with the help of your ADI) how to move the bike off and back onto its stand, and to wheel it for short distances. At this stage you need to become familiar with all of the bike's controls, especially the brakes, throttle, clutch and gears. This chapter also covers some of the basic maintenance tasks that you should be able to perform yourself.

Chapter 3, Controls and manoeuvring the motorcycle: this chapter introduces you to the basic skills of controlling the motorcycle that you will learn with the help of an ADI on a course of Initial Basic Training. They include how to start the engine and move off for the first time. By the end of this chapter you should be able to ride the motorcycle at slow speed in a traffic-free location.

Chapter 4, Gaining experience on the road: this chapter describes how you can put what you know in theory into practice in real 'on the road' practice sessions. In the beginning, you will do this under the supervision of your ADI. Later, you will do it on your own – after you have completed your course of Initial Basic Training. This chapter covers the different types of road and road layout that you will come across, and describes how you can learn to share the road safely with other road users, including motorists, cyclists and pedestrians. This chapter also covers some steering manoeuvres that you need to learn.

Chapter 5, Dealing with more challenging conditions: this chapter takes what you've learned in chapters 2, 3 and 4 and applies them to more difficult or challenging conditions – including riding in bad weather, riding at night, riding in heavy traffic and riding on different types of road. For motorcyclists who have already passed their practical test, this chapter describes some of the challenges involved in carrying a pillion passenger.

Chapter 6, Sharing the road: this chapter looks at some of the personal qualities you need to develop to become a consistently safe and competent motorcyclist. These include qualities such as being able to stay calm under pressure, to treat other road users with courtesy and respect, and to commit yourself to riding only when you are physically and mentally fit to do so safely. It also looks at things you can do to reduce the impact of your road use on the environment. Lastly it gives some tips on what to do if you are the first person on the scene of a collision.

What else you should read

Before you start to learn to ride, there's a lot you can do to prepare.

- You need to have an excellent knowledge of the *Rules of the Road*. Keep a copy handy, as you will need to refer to it often while you are learning how to ride a motorcycle.
- If you are learning to ride on your own motorcycle or on that of a family member or friend, make sure to get familiar yourself with its user manual or handbook.
- The RSA publishes leaflets on a wide range of topics relating to road safety and driver licensing. These are available in public libraries, post offices, garda stations and other public places.
- The RSA website is packed with resources for learner drivers and motorcyclists. These include tips and hints on road safety, information about the driving tests and lists of Approved Driving Instructors for every county. You can also download the *Rules of the Road* and other documents from the website. And, you can also look at road safety videos.

1. Getting yourself organised

In this chapter

The focus of this chapter is to help you organise the programme of learning that you need to follow to become a safe and competent motorcyclist.

- You need to take a course of Initial Basic Training under the supervision of an Approved Driving Instructor (ADI);
- You need to record your own progress, and make commitments to riding a motorcycle in a responsible way;
- You need to know about the legal and safety requirements that you must follow as a motorcyclist.

Before you start

You must hold a valid learner permit for the category of motorcycle you are going to learn on. To obtain a learner permit, you must first pass the driver theory test for motorcycles.

You and your Approved Driving Instructor (ADI)

While you are learning to ride a motorcycle, you need to take an approved course of Initial Basic Training (IBT) from an IBT-registered Approved Driving Instructor (ADI) specialised in motorcycles.

Motorcycle ADIs have a wealth of experience and knowledge about riding motorcycles and they know how to pass on their expertise to learner riders. A course of Initial Basic Training follows a standard syllabus established by the RSA. During the course, you will learn the basics of motorcycle riding in a safe and controlled environment. The course includes a mixture of classroom, training ground and on-the-road instruction, and it takes 16 hours in total.

Once you complete the course, you receive an Initial Basic Training Certificate of Completion, which you should keep with your learner permit. **You may not ride unsupervised on a public road before you receive your Certificate.**

Your ADI is the expert to whom you should direct any questions that you have about riding. The RSA website includes a list of all registered ADIs, sorted by county, and the RSA recommends that you continue to take lessons from an ADI after your Initial Basic Training.

See **www.rsa.ie/RSA/Learner-Drivers/Safe-Driving/Find-an-instructor/**

Learning and doing

Learning to ride a motorcycle is a serious undertaking. There are so many things to learn and remember, and so many things to do and practise. You want to learn and practise within a structured environment that will help you to develop good and safe riding habits.

Apart from learning the skills of controlling the motorcycle, you need to develop a wide range of skills, such as:

- Observation skills – that enable you to take notice of what other road users are doing or are about to do;
- Judgement skills – that enable you to know what's the right thing to do in different circumstances;
- Planning skills – that help you to prepare for different manoeuvres and routes;
- Anticipation skills – that help you to avoid hazards; and
- Reaction skills – that enable you to take evasive action in the event of a dangerous situation or an emergency.

Facts about motorcycles

Motorcycles represent less than 2% of licensed vehicles in Ireland. However deaths of motorcyclists account for 10% of all road deaths.

Motorcyclists are six times more likely to be killed on Irish roads than any other road user.

Competencies: things to know and things to do

To become a safe and competent motorcyclist, there are things you need to know and things you need to do:

Things you need to know	Things you need to do
The things you need to know include:	The things you need to do include:
<ul><li>Rules and regulations, including the Rules of the Road and the rules governing the learner permit;</li><li>Bike control, safety and maintenance tasks: how the bike works and the correct way to use its controls;</li><li>Showing consideration for other road users, particularly vulnerable road users; and</li><li>How to recognise, manage and avoid risk.</li></ul>	<ul><li>Manoeuvring your bike and using all its controls competently;</li><li>Practising your riding skills within a structured programme;</li><li>Controlling and manoeuvring the bike in traffic;</li><li>Planning ahead, including use of maps and other navigation aids; and</li><li>Riding at night and in other challenging conditions.</li></ul>

The things you learn and the things you do go hand in hand and influence each other. The theory you learn informs how you ride; and your driving practice makes sense of the theory you have learnt. Mastery of the theory and practice together help you to develop the good habits of safe and competent motorcycling.

My commitment: 1
I am willing to learn how to ride a motorcycle in a structured and controlled way with the help of a registered ADI. I will follow a course of Initial Basic Training.

Signed (Learner)

Recording your progress: making commitments

When you learn to ride a motorcycle, you learn to take responsibility. This includes taking responsibility for keeping track of your own learning and being honest with yourself about the progress you are making.

Throughout this book there are '**My commitment**' panels where you are invited to sign off on areas of competence or knowledge that you have mastered. These cover most of the theory, practice and good habits that you need to learn in order to become a safe and competent motorcyclist. By signing off on these, you are affirming that:

- ⊙ You have mastered a particular area of competence or knowledge;
- ⊙ You understand the risks and hazards relating to that competence; and
- ⊙ You are making a commitment about your own behaviour as a motorcyclist.

Signing off on commitments

Don't sign off on a commitment until you're fully confident that you have mastered the competence or knowledge it relates to. If you feel you're close but not quite there on a particular area, ask your ADI for advice. For example, you can focus on that area during your next session. For convenience the 'My commitment' panels are also included at the back of this book.

My commitment: 2
I will assess my own learning progress critically and honestly and will sign off on a topic only when I am confident I have mastered it fully.
Signed (Learner)

Learning in a structured way

Developing the full range of motorcycling skills takes time and patience. The best way to learn is within a structured environment, with the help of an Approved Driving Instructor (ADI). Just like any other task, you will want the best possible coaching to ensure that you start off in the correct way and develop good habits as you learn. Bad habits can be very hard to 'unlearn'; and they also make it much more difficult to pass the practical motorcycle test.

Good road conditions

When you have developed the range of skills to a satisfactory level, you can do the practical test. Passing the practical motorcycle test, however, does not mean that you are an expert motorcyclist – even the most 'experienced' rider can be a learner at times – for example in challenging on-road conditions such as those brought on by snow, fog or very heavy rain.

Wet conditions

Different weather conditions can require different riding behaviour.

Snow / icy conditions

My commitment: 3

I understand the responsibility of taking a motorcycle onto the road and of sharing the road with other people. I am ready to take on that personal responsibility and to take ownership of how I learn to ride a motorcycle.

Signed (Learner)

Stages in learning to ride

When you're learning to ride a motorcycle you progress through several different stages. All the time, you're adding to your knowledge, growing in competence, and developing good habits. For most learners, these stages can be summarised as follows:

Stage	Description
1. First steps	At the beginning you have to take in a lot of new information and develop new skills. When you are riding a motorcycle, you have to keep all this information in your head, to pick out the bits that are relevant at any time, and to apply that information to the task in hand. This can be hard and you should not expect to achieve too much too quickly.
2. Developing skills and gaining experience	At this stage you still have to go through the same process of selecting information, but you will be getting better at knowing what is relevant in any situation, and you'll be getting more comfortable with the skills needed.
3. Mastering skills and acquiring confidence	By now, figuring out what to do in any situation will be almost automatic. You will be reacting appropriately to situations as they arise without seeming to think about them.

What you need to progress

To progress through these three stages, you need the right information, the right coaching and the right experience. A good motorcyclist is a confident motorcyclist; but an over-confident motorcyclist might not always judge situations accurately.

A course of Initial Basic Training with an approved ADI will set you on the right road to becoming a safe and competent motorcyclist.

The learner motorcyclist and the law

Before you ride a motorcycle on the public road, you need to make sure that you are legal in every way:

- Your motorcycle must be insured and you must be insured to ride it;
- Your motorcycle must be taxed;
- You must have an up-to-date learner permit – see **Getting your learner permit** below;
- To practise unsupervised on the public road, you must have an Initial Basic Training Certificate of Completion;
- You must not carry a passenger if you hold a learner permit as this is a penal offence;
- You must wear a safety helmet; and
- While you are the holder of a learner permit, you must wear a reflective yellow tabard with L-plates front and rear. Once of the advantages of displaying L-plates is that other road users may be more considerate towards you if they know you are a learner.

Getting your learner permit

Before you can get a learner permit, you must pass a theory test. See www.theorytest.ie for more information on how to apply for the theory test.

- Application forms for learner permits are available at Garda stations and at local Motor Tax offices.
- You must be at least 16 years old to apply for a learner permit, and you must be normally resident in Ireland.
- The first time you apply for a learner permit you must also supply a satisfactory eyesight report completed by a registered ophthalmic optician or by a doctor.
- A learner permit is normally valid for two years from the date of issue.

Learner permit categories

Category	Description	Minimum age
A	Motorcycle with maximum power output of 25kW or a power/weight ratio of 0.16 kW per kg.	18
A1	Motorcycle with a maximum engine capacity of 125cc or less, and a power output of 11kW or less.	16
M	Moped with a maximum design speed of 45 km/hour or less.	16

To ride a more powerful motorcycle, you must have held a full category A licence for at least two years.

Staying safe

Get into the habit of 'thinking safe' at all times.

- Always wear your helmet, protective clothing and protective footwear.
- Never ride a motorcycle while under the influence of alcohol or drugs (legal or illegal). If you are convicted of a drink-related offence, you will be automatically disqualified from riding a motorcycle or driving for up to six years, and you could face a jail sentence if you are involved in a serious collision. If you are on prescribed medication, ask your doctor if this is likely to affect your riding.
- You need to be fully alert when you are riding a motorcycle, so don't ride when you are very tired. Tiredness is a factor in many road collisions.

The *Rules of the Road* includes detailed information about getting a learner permit.

My commitment: 4

I understand the legal issues relating to riding a motorcycle and I commit myself to safe and responsible practice.

Signed (Learner)

2. Getting started

In this chapter

At this stage you have a motorcycle learner permit and you have arranged to take a course of Initial Basic Training with a registered ADI. This chapter moves on to cover:

- How to choose a motorcycle that is suitable for your needs;
- The importance of having the right safety equipment and protective clothing;
- How to take the bike off and put it back on its stand, mount and dismount, and wheel it a short distance;
- Your motorcycle's basic controls – especially the brakes, throttle, steering, clutch and gears; and
- Basic regular maintenance tasks that you need to know how to do.

These topics will be covered by the ADI during your course of Initial Basic Training.

The right motorcycle for you

Choosing the right motorcycle for you depends on many things, some of which come down to personal preference, lifestyle and the type of riding you will be doing. The range of bikes available is huge, from mopeds, scooters and city bikes, to sport bikes, touring bikes and off-roaders. A 1,000cc bike that is suitable for long-distance touring might not be very suitable on short commuting trips; while a 50cc moped might not be strong enough on rural back roads.

When choosing a bike, you need to think of performance, comfort, the cost of insurance and fuel efficiency.

Riding a motorcycle is much more physically demanding than driving a car, so whichever type of bike you choose, you need to make sure that it 'fits' you well and that you can stay in full control at all times. Not all motorcycles are adjustable for people of different height and reach. You need to make sure that:

- Both of your feet reach the ground, and that you can balance the bike with one foot on the ground;
- You can reach the handlebars and controls comfortably;
- The sitting position is comfortable and you can ride without putting a strain on your back; and
- You are strong enough to move the bike on and off its stand and to wheel it short distances.

Why you need the right protective clothing

As a motorcyclist you are among the most vulnerable road users. On two wheels you don't have the same stability as you would in a car and you don't have as much protection in the event of a collision. Most road collisions involving cars are relatively minor, as long the car is travelling at a slow speed and the driver and all passengers are wearing seat belts. By contrast, every motorcycle collision is potentially very serious.

No matter who is at fault in a collision, a motorcyclist is likely to come off worst. If you fall from or are thrown from your bike, even at slow speed, at the very least you will be badly bruised. From the very start of your motorcycling career, make sure that you have the right protective clothing, so that:

- You are likely to be less seriously injured if you are involved in a collision;
- You will be more comfortable and better protected against the weather; and
- You will be more easily seen by other road users.

During your Initial Basic Training, your ADI will not permit you to ride unless you have all the appropriate protective clothing and equipment. The ADI will also explain to you in more detail the importance of having the right personal protective equipment (PPE).

You need to wear the right protective clothing no matter what kind of motorcycle you are riding. The rain and cold will affect you just as much on a small-engined moped as on a large touring bike, and your body is just as vulnerable whatever kind of bike you fall off.

But it's so expensive!

Do not be tempted to buy substandard protective clothing or equipment. What price your life? Your mobility? Your ability to work? A good helmet and protective clothing are sound investments that could prevent serious injury or save your life.

Safety helmet

You must wear a properly fastened safety helmet when riding a motorcycle. This is your best protection against head and neck injury if you are involved in a collision – the majority of serious and fatal motorcycle collisions involve these sorts of injuries.

Choosing a helmet

Buy a **new** helmet from a reputable dealer. Do not be tempted to buy a second-hand helmet or to borrow someone else's helmet. The new helmet you buy should be to an approved quality standard such as those of UNECE or should carry the British Standards Institute's 'kitemark'. There are two main types of helmet:

- Full-face helmets have chin protection and a hinged visor. They give more protection in the event of a collision and also give more weather protection. Keep the visor down while you are riding.
- Open face helmets do not have chin protection and should be worn with a separate visor or goggles. These are preferred by riders who feel 'closed in' by a full-face helmet.

Helmets come in a wide range of sizes – make sure to get one that fits you snugly all the way around and is not loose. When you are wearing your helmet, make sure that it is properly fastened. If you have a collision, a loose or badly-fitting helmet will probably fly off and give you no protection.

Maintenance of your helmet

There are some regular cleaning and maintenance checks that you should do on your helmet.

- Check your helmet regularly for any obvious defects such as scratches or cracks, loose padding or frayed straps. Do not use a helmet that has been dropped or bashed around – you might not be able to see hairline cracks or other faults in the helmet. If in doubt, buy a new helmet.
- Follow the manufacturer's instructions for cleaning your helmet. Do not use petrol or any solvents, as these could damage the surface of the helmet.

Visor and goggles

If you use an open-face helmet, then you should also wear a visor or goggles. As with the helmet, goggles and visors should be to an approved standard, such as those of UNECE or the British Standards Institute. Follow these maintenance guidelines for all visors and goggles.

- Keep the visor or goggles clean so that you have a clear view of the road while you are riding.
- Follow the manufacturer's instructions for washing them – for most types, warm soapy water is good. Do not use petrol or harsh solvents.
- Do not use a tinted visor or goggles in poor light or at night.
- Scratches on your visor or goggles can obscure your view, or increase the dazzle of oncoming headlights or contribute to glare if you are facing into a low sun – if your visor or goggles become scratched or damaged, replace them.

Protective clothing

When you are riding a motorcycle you are very exposed to the elements, and travelling at even moderate speeds exaggerates the effects of cold and 'wind chill'. For these reasons, having the right clothing is essential. Good quality protective clothing will help to keep you warm and dry, and it will also offer you greater protection in the event of a collision.

There is a wide range of protective clothing available. You can choose clothing made from hi-tech synthetic materials with weather-proof features, or you can go for the traditional leather look which has been popular with generations of bikers. Whichever type you buy, make sure it fits you well and that it is reinforced at vulnerable points, shoulders, knees, elbows and hips.

As with your helmet, don't be tempted to buy cheap or substandard protective clothing.

Clothing to be seen in

While you are riding on a learner's permit, you must wear a fluorescent yellow tabard with L-plates front and rear.

Making sure that other road users see you is an essential part of safe riding. Wear fluorescent orange or yellow clothing, such as a tabard or overjacket. These should also have reflective strips to make you more visible at night.

Protective gloves

Strong protective gloves are an essential part of any motorcyclist's kit. If you ever fall off your bike, you will instinctively put your hands down to break your fall – and you could do serious damage to your hands. Protective gloves will help prevent serious injury. They will also give you good protection against cold and rain and enable you to operate the hand controls easily.

Protective footwear

Protective motorcycle boots will help keep your feet warm and dry and will also give you protection in the event of a collision.

My commitment: 5

I understand the importance of wearing a securely fastened safety helmet and appropriate protective clothing.

I will never ride a motorcycle without adequate protective clothing and a safety helmet.

I will maintain my protective clothing and helmet in good condition.

Signed (Learner)

Without Protective Equipment | *With Protective Equipment*

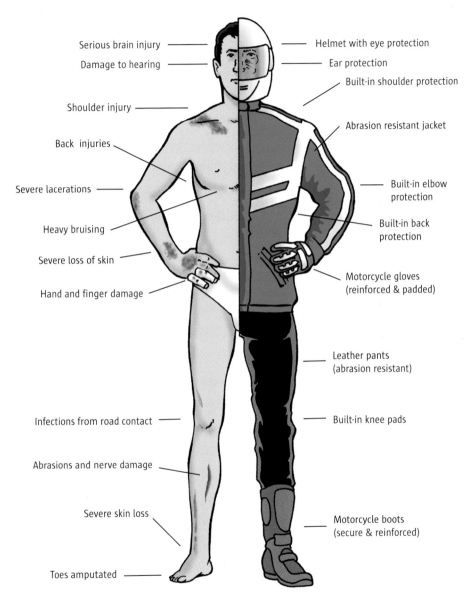

Serious brain injury ⸺ ⸺ Helmet with eye protection

Damage to hearing ⸺ ⸺ Ear protection

Built-in shoulder protection

Shoulder injury ⸺

Abrasion resistant jacket

Back injuries

Severe lacerations ⸺ ⸺ Built-in elbow protection

Heavy bruising ⸺ Built-in back protection

Severe loss of skin ⸺

Hand and finger damage ⸺ ⸺ Motorcycle gloves (reinforced & padded)

Leather pants (abrasion resistant)

Infections from road contact ⸺ ⸺ Built-in knee pads

Abrasions and nerve damage ⸺

Severe skin loss ⸺ ⸺ Motorcycle boots (secure & reinforced)

Toes amputated ⸺

Based on the Transport Accident Commission, Austraila, 2001

Know your bike – before you turn on the engine

Before you take a motorcycle onto the public road, you need to be totally familiar with all the controls. Modern motorcycles are complex machines with a lot of controls and other features that you need to know about and learn how to use.

During the course of Initial Basic Training, your ADI will show you all the controls on your motorcycle. For convenience, these can be broken down into the following:

- Foot controls;
- Instruments;
- Controls on the left handlebar;
- Controls on the right handlebar.

You need to be totally familiar with all the bike's controls without having to look for them while you are on the road.

See also

The controls on your motorcycle will be similar to but probably not exactly the same as those described in this chapter. Check your motorcycle manual for details of all the controls on your bike.

Foot controls

On most modern motorcycles, you change gears with your left foot and operate the rear brake with your right foot.

Gear selector

Lift up the gear selector with the upper part of your foot to change up a gear; and press down with the sole of your foot to change down a gear. On most bikes, FIRST gear is the lowest position, with NEUTRAL above it, and then SECOND, THIRD, FOURTH and FIFTH (where provided).

Without turning on the engine, practise letting the clutch in and out (very slowly and smoothly) and changing up and down through the gears.

Your ADI will show you how to use the gears during your Initial Basic Training.

Rear brake

The rear brake pedal is on the right side, just in front of the footrest.

Practise moving your right foot onto the brake pedal.

Note   On many mopeds, scooters and semi-automatic motorcycles, the rear brake is on the left handlebar – if you are unsure, ask your ADI for advice.

Instruments

You need to know about all the devices on the instrument panel – what they're for and how to use them. On most motorcycles, these include the following:

Meters	These include the speedometer, odometer, trip meter, rev counter and fuel gauge.
Warning lights	These are lights that give you information about serious faults or the status of certain items. They include the NEUTRAL light, indicator lights, headlight ON lights (dipped and full), temperature gauge, oil pressure warning light and so on.
Ignition switch	Use this switch to start the engine. See page 31 for a guide to starting up.

If you are not sure what any of the controls or instruments are for, or if you don't know how they work, ask your ADI to show you or explain their functions.

Left-hand handlebar controls – **typical layout**

Clutch lever

This lever engages and disengages the clutch. When you pull the clutch lever towards you, you disengage the engine from the rear wheel. You need to do this when you are changing gear, and to prevent the bike from stalling when you come to a stop.

Control of the clutch and coordination of clutch and gears is covered in chapter 3.

Choke

You use the choke when you are starting the bike from cold. The purpose of the choke is to change the mix of fuel and air supplied to the engine. Once the engine has warmed up, you should turn the choke off – otherwise you're using more fuel than you need to and you might be causing the engine to 'race'. Many bikes now have an automatic choke.

Indicators

Use these to indicate when you are turning left or right. Not all bikes have self-cancelling indicators, so be sure to turn the indicator off after you have made a turn.

Horn

Your horn is an essential safety feature of your motorcycle. You might need to use it in an emergency to let other road users know you are there.

Headlight dip control

Use this to lower your main headlight when required.

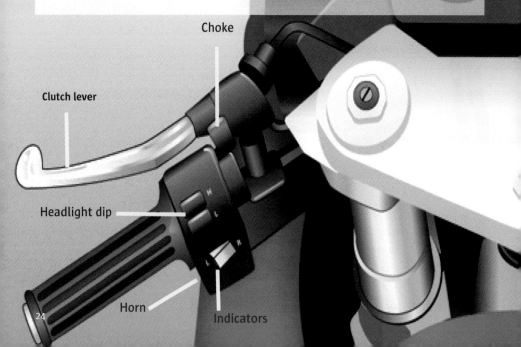

Choke

Clutch lever

Headlight dip

Horn

Indicators

Right-hand handlebar controls – **typical layout**

Throttle (accelerator)

Twist the throttle towards you to increase the flow of fuel to the engine and so increase speed. Twist it away from you to reduce speed. When you release the throttle, it returns to a resting position

Front brake lever

This lever operates the front brake and also turns on your rear-facing brake light to let following traffic know that you are braking.

Electric starter

Use this switch to start the engine. See page 32 for a guide to starting up.

Engine cut-out switch (kill switch)

Press this switch to turn off the engine and all electric circuits in the event of an emergency.

Light switch

This has three positions: off, parking light and headlight. The control for changing between full and dipped beam is on the left handlebar.

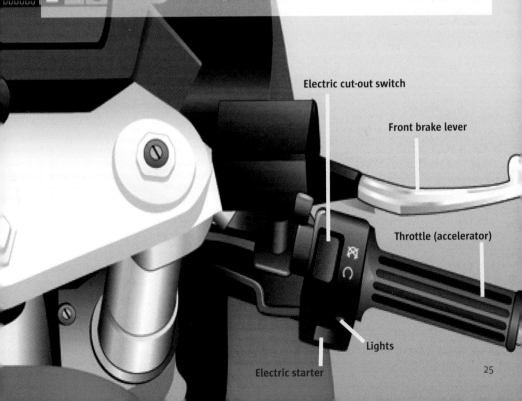

Electric cut-out switch

Front brake lever

Throttle (accelerator)

Lights

Electric starter

My commitment: 6

I have studied all the motorcycle's controls and instruments. I know the purpose of each instrument and can operate each control.

Signed (Learner)

Using the stand

When it is parked, your motorcycle is supported by a stand – either a centre stand or a side stand.

During your Initial Basic Training, your ADI will show you how to move the motorcycle off and onto its stands safely, and how to avoid personal injury or damage to the bike while you are doing so.

Safety first

Before you move off, make sure that the stand is fully tucked up under the bike.

When parking your bike, make sure that the ground is level and the surface is firm.

Centre stand

To take a motorcycle off a centre stand, follow these steps:

1	Place yourself to the left of the bike, with your left foot slightly to the left of the stand.
2	Place your left hand on the left-hand handlebar and your right hand on the frame near the saddle.
3	Pull the motorcycle forward off its stand, and put your right hand on the front brake (right-hand handlebar) to keep control of the bike.

To place a motorcycle on a centre stand, follow these steps:

1	Place yourself to the left of the bike, with your left hand on the left handlebar and your right hand on the frame near the saddle.
2	Push the stand down with your right foot.
3	While holding your foot against the stand, pull the bike backwards onto the stand.

Side stand

To take a motorcycle off a side stand, follow these steps:

1	Place yourself to the left of the bike, with your left hand on the left handlebar and your right hand on the frame near the saddle.
2	Push the motorcycle upright so that it is no longer supported by the stand.
3	Push the stand firmly up with your foot and make sure it locks into place.

To place a motorcycle on a side stand, follow these steps:

1	Place yourself to the left of the bike, with your left hand on the left handlebar and your right hand on the frame near the saddle.
2	With the motorcycle upright, pull the stand down with your foot.
3	Let the motorcycle lean towards you until its weight is supported by the stand.

Mounting and dismounting

When mounting, stand to the left of the motorcycle and apply the front brake with your right hand. Then, with your weight on your left leg, throw your right leg over the bike and sit on the saddle. Place your feet on the ground to maintain balance.

Mounting and dismounting from the left means that you are usually doing it on the side away from the traffic. Practise mounting and dismounting until you find it easy.

When dismounting, pay attention to the difference in level between the road and the kerb, and be careful of slippery underfoot surfaces – such as loose gravel.

Practise mounting and dismounting with the motorcycle off its stand.

Sitting on the motorcycle

While you are sitting on the bike, make sure that you can reach all of the controls comfortably – your elbows should be slightly bent, and your arms should not be at full stretch. You should be able to place both of your feet on the ground while the bike is stationary, and you should be able to balance the bike with one foot on the ground and the other on the footrest or on the gear selector (left foot) or rear brake (right foot).

Each time you sit on the motorcycle, check that the mirrors give the best possible rear view on either side, and adjust as necessary.

Walking with the motorcycle

One of the skills that you need to master is that of wheeling your motorcycle with the engine turned off and the gears in **neutral**. During your course of Initial Basic Training, your ADI will show you how the wheel the bike safely.

Take the bike off its stand and hold it with both hands on the handlebars. Keep your right hand lightly on the front brake to control the bike so that it doesn't run away from you. Lean the bike slightly towards you so that it is easier to balance. Look ahead while you are wheeling the bike – not at the ground, and make sure that you keep the bike well balanced.

Practise wheeling the bike until you have mastered it.

My commitment: 7
I know how to take the motorcycle on and off its stand, can mount and dismount easily, and can wheel the bike with the engine turned off.
Signed (Learner)

Carrying out basic technical checks on your motorcycle

You are responsible for ensuring that your motorcycle is maintained in a safe and roadworthy condition.

A well-maintained bike will be safer, more efficient and less likely to break down, so you should make sure that your bike is serviced regularly. Items such as spark plugs and the air filter will need to be changed from time to time; and the carburettor and ignition settings will need to be adjusted.

In between services, there are some basic checks that you can do yourself. This includes basic checks for the following, P-O-W-D-E-R:

- **P**etrol (fuel)
- **O**il
- **W**ater (coolant)
- **D**amage
- **E**lectrics
- **R**ubber (tyres)

Basic checks for all of these are described below. Ask your ADI to run through these checks with you at least once, so that you know what you need to do on a regular basis.

Petrol (fuel)

The one basic maintenance task you will have to do regularly is to put fuel in your motorcycle. Petrol is highly flammable, so be very careful when you're filling up. You also need to know what type of fuel your bike takes:

O Most motorcycles have four-stroke engines and take standard petrol as fuel.

O Some motorcycles have two-stroke engines and take a mixture of petrol and oil, usually in a ratio of 20:1 – your user manual will give you the exact ratio for your bike. On most modern two-stroke bikes, the oil is stored in a separate tank which you will need to top up from time to time.

Oil

Lubricating oil plays a key role in keeping your engine running smoothly, and you need to check the oil level regularly. Park your bike on level ground when you are checking the oil level. You should always check the oil before a long journey. Ask your ADI to show you where the dipstick is on your motorcycle.

1	Remove the dipstick and wipe it with a clean cloth.
2	Reinsert the dipstick and then remove it again.
3	The oil should be between the MIN and MAX markers on the dipstick.

If the oil is below the MIN marker, you need to top it up. Use the grade of oil recommended by your bike's manufacturer. Don't fill above the MAX marker.

Water (coolant)

The engine of your bike is either air-cooled or liquid-cooled. If it is liquid-cooled, you need to check regularly that there is enough coolant liquid in the reservoir.

Do this when the engine is cool. When the engine is hot, the coolant is pressurised and could scald you if you open the reservoir.

See your manufacturer's instructions for what type of coolant to use and the level it should be at.

Damage

Get into the habit of checking your motorcycle for any damage – including the lights, body work, wheels, tyres, and the mirrors. Make sure there are no drips or leaks, or any frayed or loose cable connections.

Electrics (lights, indicators, horn)

You need to check that the horn and all the lights on your motorcycle are functioning correctly:

- Headlights (full and dipped)
- Brake lights
- Parking lights
- Indicators (front and rear)

See your motorcycle's user manual for instructions on how to change the light bulbs.

Rubber (tyres)

Your tyres are in direct contact with the road, and maintaining your tyres is essential for safe and economical driving. Get into the habit of checking your tyres regularly.

- Keep an eye out for any bumps, bulges or tears on the surface or side walls of the tyres.
- Make sure that the surface of the tyres is not worn and that they have adequate tread depth.
- Incorrectly inflated tyres can be dangerous, so you should check the tyre pressure regularly.

Other checks

Your ADI will also show you other checks that you need to carry out, including:

- The brakes – for proper adjustment and operation;
- The steering head (where the front fork meets the frame) – for wear and adjustment;
- The suspension – for any obvious faults. If the suspension is too soft, you won't have enough compression on rough ground or bumpy roads; if it is too hard, you might get too much rebound; and
- All nuts, bolts and pins – make sure they are securely in place.

My commitment: 8

I have a good understanding of the basic service and maintenance requirements of my motorcycle and can carry out basic maintenance and safety checks myself.

Signed (Learner)

3. Controls and manoeuvring the motorcycle

In this chapter

At this stage you know quite a lot about your motorcycle, but you have not yet put any of your knowledge into practice.

This chapter moves on to describe how you can start to learn the basic skills that you need to ride a motorcycle – starting the engine for the first time, moving off and stopping the bike. You will learn the basic skills as part of your Initial Basic Training under the supervision of an ADI.

By the end of this chapter you will be able to control the motorcycle at low speeds in a safe, traffic-free environment. You will then be ready to begin on-the-road practice with your ADI.

Starting and stopping the bike: the first time

Up to now, you've been acquiring knowledge about your motorcycle. Now it's time to actually begin to do something – to start the bike, move off and then stop.

Moving off is probably the most difficult manoeuvre that you will learn. You need to learn to control the clutch by slowly releasing it while at the same time putting gentle pressure on the throttle and gently releasing the rear brake. Once you are moving, you will find that controlling a moving motorcycle requires considerable balance and coordination.

During your course of Initial Basic Training, your ADI will be with you to make sure that you learn how to start and stop the bike in a safe way.

Manual or automatic

The procedures described below deal with motorcycles with manual transmission – that is, bikes on which you have to change the gears manually, with the aid of a clutch.

Some motorcycles, including many mopeds and scooters, have automatic or semi-automatic transmission (with no clutch lever).

If you pass your motorcycle practical test on an automatic motorcycle, then you will only be licensed to ride automatic motorcycles.

Starting the engine

There is quite a lot of variation in the start-up procedures of different motorcycles. Some use a kickstarter, others use an electric starter. Some won't start unless the gear selector is in **neutral**; for others you need to check that **neutral** is selected. And on some bikes you have to turn the fuel tap to open the flow of fuel to the engine.

For most makes and models, the procedures are as follows – your ADI will show you if there are any variations with your bike.

1.	Take the bike off its stand and mount it.
2.	Check that the gear selector is in **neutral**. If you are not sure, rock the bike forward – if the back wheel moves freely, then you are in **neutral** . *If the bike is not in **neutral** when you start, it could jerk forward when you start it, which might be dangerous.* Insert the ignition key and turn it **on**. The green **N** light should come on to indicate that the bike is in **neutral**.
3.	If your bike has a fuel tap, turn it **on**.
4.	If you are starting the bike from cold, turn **on** the choke (where fitted). You don't need to do this if your bike has an automatic choke.
5.	Check that the engine cut-out switch is turned **off**.
6.	Apply the front brake.

7	**Electric starter** Press the starter button and release it when the engine starts up.	**Kick starter** Fold down the kick-starter and press down on it with your foot, allowing it to spring back as the engine starts up. Fold the kick starter back to its normal position once the engine is running.

8	Twist the throttle gently towards you to increase the engine speed. The engine should settle to a steady hum. Remember to turn off the choke once the engine has warmed up – a minute or two should be enough.

Moving off and stopping

Moving off and stopping for the first time is not easy, and the only way you'll learn it is to do it. When you are on a course of basic instruction, your ADI will ensure that you are on level ground in a safe location and can do no harm, to yourself or anyone else. Your ADI will also make sure that you understand the basics of stopping the bike safely before you move off.

Moving off

Moving off requires very fine control of the clutch lever, throttle and rear brake. Avoid jerky or sudden movements of the controls so that you don't jerk forward or cut out (stall). You also need to let each of your feet take your weight at different times.

1.	Start the engine as described above, and place your right foot on the ground to take your weight. Keep the front brake pulled in to hold the bike steady before you move off.
2.	Pull in (squeeze) the clutch lever all the way.
3.	Select FIRST gear, and then put your left foot on the ground so that it takes your weight..
4.	Put your right foot on the footrest and apply the rear brake – you can now release the front brake.
5.	Very gradually release the clutch until you feel the 'bite point' – this is when you feel the bike beginning to move. Hold the bike momentarily in this position, gradually twist the throttle towards you and continue to release the clutch gradually
6.	As the bike begins to move forward, release the rear brake smoothly and continue to accelerate gently.
7.	As you are moving, bring your left foot up onto the footrest.

Moving off facing uphill

If you are moving off while facing uphill (for example, at traffic lights), you will need to give a little more throttle and be very careful when you release the rear brake.

- If you release the rear brake too soon, you risk rolling backwards; and
- If you release it too late, you risk jerking forward or stalling.

Stopping

You need to be able to stop your bike smoothly and promptly. As with moving off, smooth and gentle use of the controls will ensure that the engine doesn't stall.

1.	Release the throttle.
2.	Gently apply the brakes.
3.	Just before you come to a stop, pull in the clutch lever to stop the engine from cutting out
4.	As you come to a stop, place your left foot on the ground to take your weight.
5.	Keep the front brake applied while you release the rear brake and place your right foot on the ground.
6.	Bring your left foot back up onto the footrest and change to NEUTRAL – you can now release the clutch.

Practice tip

Moving off and stopping are essential skills for the motorcyclist. Practise these over and over until you are confident you can do it without stalling or jerking forward. As you practise, try to concentrate on the following:

○ Keeping your balance as you ride in a straight line at slow speed;

○ Coordinating the controls as you move;

○ Keeping the rear brake covered;

○ Keeping both your feet on the foot pegs while you are moving – place your left foot on the ground just before you stop; and

○ Using the controls (throttle, clutch and brakes) smoothly.

My commitment: 9

I am able to start the engine of the motorcycle, move off and stop safely in a traffic-free location.

Signed (Learner)

Moving off from the kerb

As you practise starting and moving off, get into the habit of checking your mirrors, signalling and checking your blind spots before you actually move off. This is the **Observation – Signal – Observation (blind spots) – Manoeuvre** routine.

Observation
Take an observation of what's happening around you and look in your mirrors to check that it is safe to move out.

Signal
Signal your intention to move by turning on an indicator.

Observation (blind spots)
Before you move off, check your mirrors again and check over your shoulder for your blind spots – motorcyclists call this look 'the life saver'.

Manoeuvre
Move off from the kerb when you are satisfied it is safe to do so.

Steering

As on a bicycle, you use the handlebars to control the direction of the motorcycle. Hold the handlebars with both hands, firmly but not too tightly.

As you are practising moving off and riding short distances, get used to the feel of how the bike responds to the steering adjustments you make. You'll soon be able to make very precise adjustments in the steering. Practise steering the bike to very precise positions at low speed over and over.

At higher speeds the feel (or dynamics) of steering changes and you need to lean your body in the direction you wish to go – for example, as you go round a bend. The faster you are travelling and the sharper the bend, the more you will have to lean. After you have completed the bend, bring the bike back to the upright position.

Changing up to second gear ...

You use first gear when you are moving off. As you increase your speed you change up through the gears.

Second and third gears are intermediate gears and you use them in slower-moving traffic.

Once you are reasonably well practised at starting, moving off and stopping, you can learn how to change up to second gear. This requires coordination between both of your hands and your left foot. Follow these steps:

1.	Ease off the throttle.
2.	Pull in the clutch fully with your left hand, and put the gear lever into SECOND gear with your left foot.
3.	Very gradually release the clutch lever with your left hand while at the same time twisting gently on the throttle. Listen to how the engine sound changes when you change gear.

... and to third gear and beyond

To change up to third gear, you follow the same steps as for changing into second, except that you put the gear lever into the third gear position. You can do this later when you are driving on the open road. And you can follow the same steps for changing up to fourth and fifth gears.

My commitment: 10
I am able to ride the motorcycle in a traffic-free location and can change gears.
Signed (Learner)

Slowing down, braking, stopping

While you are learning to ride, one of the most important skills you need to master is how to slow down, brake and bring your bike to a stop. Your bike has front and rear brakes and you need to learn how to use them on their own and together.

In general, the front brake is more effective and in normal road conditions you should use it before you use the rear brake. (This is not what you might expect if you have experience riding a bicycle.)

Aim to brake early and progressively – in other words, don't wait until just before you need to stop to use the brakes. It is better not to brake while the bike is leaning – for example, when you are going around a bend. Progressive braking means that you start by braking gently and then gradually increase the pressure, so that your braking is never jerky.

1.	Slow down in advance by releasing the throttle – in low gears this will slow the bike a lot.
2.	Pull gently on the front brake and then press gently on the rear brake.
3.	Pull more firmly on the front brake and press the rear brake firmly to come to a complete stop.
4.	Just before you come to a complete stop, pull in the clutch so that the engine does not cut out.

When you brake, the weight of the bike is transferred to the front wheel which then has a better grip on the road surface. At the same time, the rear wheel has less grip – so if you press the rear brake too firmly, you risk locking the rear wheel.

Practice tip

It is almost always better to use both brakes to bring the bike to a stop, but the exact combination to use depends on things such as the speed you are riding at and the road surface.

You need to develop a sense of how each of the brakes works, how to control them, and how they work in combination with each other. Your aim should be to learn what is the best way to combine the two brakes safely in any situation.

Your ADI will give you guidance on the combination of front and rear brakes to use in different situations.

Variations

Some motorcycles have 'linked' braking systems where when you pull the front brake, the rear brake is also used to give more efficient braking. This is sometimes combined with antilock braking systems (ABS) that are designed to help your tyres keep their grip when you are braking very hard.

If your bike has these features, you should be aware of them and the way they affect how you brake. Talk to your ADI about this, and read what your bike's manual has to say about braking.

My commitment: 11
I understand the way that the front and rear brakes work, and I know how to use them in combination to slow down and stop.
Signed (Learner)

4. Gaining experience on the road

In this chapter

Your first experience on the public road will be under the supervision of your ADI. Then, once you have the Initial Basic Training Certificate of Completion you can begin to practise on your own. This chapter sets out to help you understand the variety of challenges that you will meet in the course of your on-the-road practice. You will already be familiar with the theory of many of these challenges from your knowledge of the *Rules of the Road*. Now it's time to put what you know in theory into practice; this includes how to:

- 'Read' the road, know your position on the road; and get into the habit of following the **observation – signal – manoeuvre / position – speed – look (OSM/PSL)** routine;
- Deal safely with junctions and roundabouts, and make sure that you are in the right lane;
- Control your speed;
- Signal appropriately and understand other road users' signals; and
- Safely overtake slower-moving traffic.

This chapter also describes how you can learn balance and control manoeuvres (such as figures-of-eight, U-turns and slaloms) and practise the precise control of the brakes that you need for emergency stops.

Once you have passed your test and gained your full licence, you can ride a motorcycle on motorways – this chapter describes some of the challenges you will face in motorway riding.

Your first time on the public road

Up to now you have practised riding in very safe, traffic-free locations. You have mastered the skills of starting the bike, moving off and stopping. You are now ready to ride on the public road for the first time, in light traffic.

This is an essential part of your course of Initial Basic Training and your ADI will accompany you on another bike and will be in radio communication with you.

Combining knowledge and practice

The first time you ride a motorcycle on the public road you need to bring together all the knowledge you have gained and put it into practice. That's not as easy as it sounds. You're probably still getting used to using the bike's controls and there is so much information about the road environment to take in, think about and act upon.

On the public road

The first time you are on the public road, there are three main areas you need to concentrate on:

1.	Controlling the motorcycle and its position on the road.
2.	Obeying mandatory road signs and reading other road signs; and understanding how all road signs apply to you as a motorcyclist.
3.	Observing and anticipating what other road users are doing; and giving them advance warning of what you are going to do.

While you are riding a motorcycle on the public road, you need to:

O Observe speed limits at all times, while keeping up a speed that is safe for the road conditions and that you are comfortable with;

O Scan the road ahead and to the sides as necessary, and also keep an eye in your mirrors to check what's coming behind you; and

O Before you make manoeuvres (such as changing lane or turning at a junction), check your mirrors and blind spots, and make sure that it is safe to do the manoeuvre.

Your ADI will support and advise you throughout your first session on the road.

My commitment: 12
I am able to ride a motorcycle on the public road in a quiet location in very light traffic, with the support and advice of an ADI.
Signed (Learner)

Practice sessions

The practical, on the road element of your Initial Basic Training will take at least six hours. At the beginning, your first practice sessions will be in daylight, on quiet roads and at time when traffic is light. With the help of your ADI, you will take on more challenging journeys, and your ADI will accompany you at all times on another motorcycle.

Once you have completed the course of Initial Basic Training, the ADI will give you a Certificate of Completion. With this you can begin to practise on your own, unaccompanied. Keep the Certificate safely with your learner permit.

Varied practice journeys

Include a mix of urban, residential and rural roads in your practice. Integrate your practice journeys into your routine – for example, a trip to a supermarket, to a cinema or to a sports event could be the basis of your practice session.

Every journey you make has the potential to add valuable experience and present you with new challenges.

Plan to have at a number of journeys over the course of your learning. Your practice journeys should include all of the following:

- Turning left and right onto and off main roads
- Negotiating roundabouts
- Overtaking a slow-moving vehicle
- Starting on a hill, and riding uphill and downhill
- Urban one-way systems

- Stopping and moving off at traffic lights
- Yellow box junctions
- Changing lanes
- Stopping for pedestrians at a pedestrian crossing
- Riding around different types of bend

You will have encountered all of these already during your Initial Basic Training.

Practice tip

After each practice journey, review the challenges you faced, and identify the manoeuvres you need to practise more. Sign off on the commitments as you become competent at particular tasks or confident dealing with particular situations.

My commitment: 13

I understand the importance of planning my practice journeys in advance and gaining experience of all kinds of road challenges.

Signed (Learner)

Reading the road

As a motorcyclist on the public road, you are constantly receiving information, and you need to be able to take in this information and respond appropriately. You already know what the road signs mean from the *Rules of the Road*, but it's not always easy for learners to concentrate on riding safely and reading the road as they go.

Scan the road as you go, and get into the habit of observing changing traffic conditions and all of the information that road markings and road signs give you. It will soon become second nature for you to take in and process all the information you receive.

Road markings	Markings painted on the road surface give you a lot of complex information – for example, a solid white line in the centre of the road tells you that all traffic must keep to the left of the line, except in an emergency or for access; and a double yellow line at the side of the road tells you that you may not park there at any time.
	Also painted on the road surface are traffic lane indications and arrows, cycle lane markers, bus lane markers and direction arrows.
Yellow box junctions	You must not enter a yellow box junction unless you can clear it without stopping. An exception is when you want to turn right– in this case you may enter the box while waiting for a gap in oncoming traffic. However, you should not enter the box if it means you would block other traffic that has the right of way.
Regulatory and warning signs	Posted on the side of the road or above the road there are regulatory signs that you must obey. These include speed limits, 'Stop' and 'Yield' signs and 'No Parking' signs. Also posted along the side of the road are warning signs that tell you about junctions ahead, sharp bends, road works, and other potential hazards.
Traffic lights	You must obey all traffic lights. Where two or more sets of traffic lights are a short distance apart, be particularly careful to obey those closest to you.
Direction signs	Direction signs point the way to different places – these are found, for example, coming up to junctions and at junctions.

Learn how to distinguish between information that is relevant and information that is not relevant to you. For example, if you are going to Ballina, you might know that the turn-off you need is coming up soon, so you'll be alert for signs for Ballina and can generally ignore signs for other destinations.

Observation skills (anticipation and reaction)

Developing your skills of observation is a key part of becoming a safe and competent motorcyclist. You need to know what's going on around you at all times. Always scan the road ahead to be sure that you can anticipate situations before they become dangerous. And the faster you are travelling, the further ahead you will need to look.

Rear observation

As well as observing what's happening on the road in front of you, you also have to know what's happening behind you. Rear observation includes looking in your mirrors and turning your head to look behind.

Using your mirrors	Your mirrors are the 'eyes at the back of your head' that show you what's coming behind. Scan your mirrors regularly so you know what's going on, and always check in your mirrors before any manoeuvre such as changing lanes or turning into a different road. Be aware that your mirrors might have slightly curved glass to give you a wider field of view. This, however, will make things seem to be further away than they actually are.
Looking behind – the 'life-saver' look	Even with perfectly adjusted mirrors, there will be blind spots. These are areas behind you that you cannot see in the mirrors. You need to look over your shoulder before certain manoeuvres – for example, when you are pulling out into traffic from a parking place, or changing lanes. Make sure the road ahead is clear.

You must take effective rear observation before any manoeuvre that will affect your speed or your position on the road. Such manoeuvres include:

- Turning left or right
- Overtaking or changing lanes
- Slowing down or stopping
- Moving out into traffic
- Increasing speed
- Approaching any type of hazard

Observation–signal–manoeuvre / position–speed–look (OSM/PSL)

Every time you make a manoeuvre such as changing direction or position on the road, you should follow the OSM/PSL routine.

Observation		Take in what is happening around you on the road. Check your mirrors and your blind spots.
Signal		Signal that you intend to change position.
Manoeuvre		Do not begin the manoeuvre until you have taken good observation, have signalled your intention, and it is safe to do so. You can think of any manoeuvre as having three parts: **position–speed–look**:
	Position	Adjust your position on the road so that you will be able to carry out the manoeuvre safely.
	Speed	Adjust your speed to suit the manoeuvre, making sure you are in the right gear – for example: **○** Slow down if you are going to turn off at a junction; or **○** Accelerate if you are going to overtake another vehicle.
	Look	Look out for any potential hazards before and as you are completing the manoeuvre.

Practice tip

In the early stages of learning, practise in locations that you know, so that you won't have to worry too much about direction signs or getting lost in an unfamiliar area.

My commitment: 14

I am able to 'read the road' – to take in the information I need from changing traffic conditions, road markings, regulatory and warning signs, traffic lights, and direction signs.

Signed (Learner)

Knowing your position on the road

Knowing your position on the road and being able to steer accurately and precisely are important skills. Learning them will help you become a competent motorcyclist and help you to share the road safely with other road users.

Where lanes are not marked	Where lanes are marked
Keep to the left as you ride, but not too close to the verge or to parked cars or to the pavement (in urban areas). In wet weather avoid splashing pedestrians or cyclists.	Position your bike centrally between the lane markers. If you need to change lanes, follow the **OSM/PSL** routine. If you are going to turn off to the left or right, plan ahead so that you are in the correct lane when you arrive at the junction.

Practice tip   Observing the position of cars and other vehicles ahead of and behind you will give you a sense of where you should be on the road.

Lanes at junctions

At many junctions, road markings indicate the lanes for turning left or right or going straight. Keep to the lane for the direction you want to go in. Be particularly careful where a lane has two directional arrows – drivers or other motorcyclists in that lane might do something that you are not expecting.

Lanes on a dual carriageway

The right-hand lane on a dual carriageway is for overtaking slower-moving vehicles: it is not the 'fast lane'. Once you have overtaken the slow-moving vehicle, move back into the left lane, unless you intend overtaking another vehicle a short distance ahead.

Lanes on one-way streets

One-way streets can be confusing when you first meet them. For example, you might find yourself in a centre lane with lines of traffic passing you on both sides. Follow the road marking for the direction you wish to take and drive within the lane markers. Follow the **OSM/PSL** routine when you want to change lanes.

Keep your distance

Don't ride too close to the vehicle in front of you. The faster the traffic is moving, the greater the distance you should allow. One consequence of riding too close is that you will not be able to read road markings

The distance it will take you to stop in an emergency depends on many things, including how alert you are, the type and condition of the road surface, and how good your brakes and tyres are.

Never 'tailgate' the vehicle in front of you. If that vehicle brakes suddenly, you may be unable to avoid colliding with it.

You should leave a greater distance to the front if there is a car very close behind trying to overtake you – this will make it easier for the car behind you to overtake and then return to the left-hand lane. It will also reduce the risks associated with the overtaking driver's behaviour.

My commitment: 15

I know how to position my motorcycle on the road: I keep a safe distance between my motorcycle and the vehicle ahead; I understand how lanes work and can position my motorcycle in the appropriate lane at all times while on the road.

Signed (Learner)

Dealing with junctions

Junctions come in all shapes and sizes. Some are simple T-junctions that join country lanes to small country roads; others are busier junctions in towns (with traffic lights) and join two or more roads. Motorway interchanges are more complex, with ramped access and exit roads. Junctions are where different streams of traffic meet, and pedestrians are more likely to cross the road at a junction than anywhere else. You need to be extra careful at junctions for these reasons.

Your ADI will introduce you to most of the many different kinds of junction during your Initial Basic Training. The manoeuvres you perform should include left and right turns, crossing junctions, using filter lanes, turning at box junctions, entering and exiting roundabouts, and so on.

Stop or yield?

At most junctions the road priority is clearly indicated, and the point at which the minor road joins the major road normally shows a STOP or YIELD sign.

STOP sign
Always stop when you come to a STOP sign or Stop line (even if you can see no traffic on the major road) and yield to traffic that has the right of way.

YIELD sign
Always slow down and prepare to stop as you approach a YIELD sign. You must yield to traffic already on the major road.

Riding on a major road

When you are riding on a major road, you have priority over traffic emerging from minor roads. Signs that tell you about junctions ahead are for your information – they're not telling you to do anything, except to be careful and to be aware that cars and other traffic may be waiting to join the main road or to turn off onto the minor road.

Don't overtake in advance of a junction. A motorist turning left from a side road on your right might not have checked traffic coming from the left, and might not see you coming.

Be aware, that as a motorcyclist, you are not as visible as other road users to motorists emerging at junctions.

Joining a major road at a junction

When you approach a major road from a minor road, make sure that you stop or yield as required at the roadside sign. If there are no signs, wait at the entrance to the junction until the major road is clear and be extra careful before proceeding onto it – traffic on the major road is likely to be travelling quite fast.

- Check your mirrors and blind spots, signal in advance, and slow down as you approach the junction – follow the **OSM/PSL** routine.

- Your sight lines might not be very good as you emerge from the minor road, so look both ways before you join the major road. For example, in rural areas there could be bends or dips in the roadway or overhanging bushes that could affect your view. In towns or cities, parked cars, goods vehicles or buses setting down or taking on passengers could affect your view. Also, a slow-moving bus or lorry could hide a car that is about to overtake it.

- After you have joined the major road, accelerate to the speed appropriate for that road, but pay attention to the speed limits, traffic and other hazards on that road.

Always look both ways – even if you are turning left. An overtaking car coming from the left could be in the road space that you will be in after you make the turn. Also, a pedestrian might be crossing the main road.

Dealing with junctions

The *Rules of the Road* gives comprehensive guidance on how you should approach and behave at junctions.

Turning off a major road at a junction

Follow the **OSM/PSL** routine when you are turning off a major road at a junction; and keep these points in mind.

Turning left	Turning right
<ul><li>Check your mirrors and blind spots, signal in advance, and slow down as you approach the junction. Where possible, move closer to the left-hand side of the road or into the left turning lane where this is provided. Be particularly careful if you have to cross in front of a bus lane to turn left.</li><li>Give way to any pedestrians already crossing the minor road.</li><li>Don't cut across cyclists who are going straight ahead on the major road.</li><li>Keep to the left-hand side of the road you are joining, without swinging out over the area where cars might be waiting to emerge onto the main road.</li><li>Make sure you have selected the correct gear.</li></ul>	<ul><li>Check your mirrors and blind spots, signal in advance, and slow down as you approach the junction. Where possible, move closer to the middle of the road to enable traffic going straight on to pass you on the inside; or use the turning lane where this is provided.</li><li>If necessary, stop and wait until there is a safe gap in oncoming traffic before turning into the minor road.</li><li>Check your mirrors and blind spots again for traffic coming from behind you before you make the turn – in particular, check for any traffic that could be trying to overtake you.</li><li>Make sure there is nothing blocking your entry into the minor road that could leave you in an exposed position on the major road.</li><li>Give way to any pedestrians already crossing the minor road.</li><li>Make sure you have selected the correct gear.</li></ul>

The speed appropriate to the minor road you are joining might be much less than the speed you've been riding at on the major road.

Slip roads

Slip roads are designed to make it easy to join and leave major roads, including dual carriageways and motorways.

Joining a major road	Signal your intention to join the main road and give way to traffic already on it. Your speed should be close to that of traffic already on the main road, but not exceeding the speed limit.
Leaving a major road	Move into the correct lane well in advance of the slip road and signal your intention to leave the main road.

Junctions with traffic lights

Junctions with traffic lights can be simple or complex. Before you proceed through a green light, be sure that it applies to you. For example, at complex junctions, a green arrow might apply to traffic going straight on, but not to traffic turning left or right.

If a traffic light has been green for quite a while as you approach it, be prepared to stop when it turns amber.

If you are going straight ahead, you must wait at the edge of the yellow box junction until you are sure that you can clear the junction – even if you have a green light. If you are turning right, you may enter the yellow box junction and wait until it is safe to make the turn.

Roundabouts

A roundabout is a kind of junction where traffic moves around a central 'island'. The advantage of roundabouts over other types of junction is that traffic flows more smoothly. For the learner, roundabouts can be quite confusing. Remember the following points:

- You need to check the direction signs and road markings more carefully than usual – your exit might not be 'obvious'.
- You need to get into the correct lane depending on which exit you are taking.
- It can be difficult to see across the roundabout to where you want to go – this is particularly the case on big roundabouts with many exits.
- You can lose your sense of direction or orientation as you go around.
- You might need to cross lanes (from right to left) to get to the exit you want – while at the same time drivers or other motorcyclists are trying to cross in the opposite direction (from left to right).
- As with other busy junctions, there might be pedestrians crossing.
- You might not have to stop as you approach a roundabout, but you must yield to traffic already on the roundabout and traffic approaching from the right.

Reading the direction signs and road markings at roundabouts

Roundabouts are usually well sign-posted – both with an advance sign and signs at each exit. The advance sign shows the layout of the roundabout and where each exit leads to. You need to take note of which exit you want – first, second, third etc.

Be alert to other drivers' and motorcyclists' signals while you are on a roundabout.

In this example, the second exit is for Santry.

At the roundabout, each exit is usually marked clearly.

Exiting to the left   If your exit is to the left (9 o'clock), approach the roundabout in the left-hand lane (where there is one) and signal 'left' until you have passed through the roundabout.

Exiting straight ahead   If your exit is straight ahead (12 o'clock), approach the roundabout in the left-hand lane (where there is one) and signal 'left' after you have cleared the exit before the one you want.

Exiting to the right   If your exit is to the right (3 o'clock), approach the roundabout in the right-hand lane (where there is one), and indicate right. On a multiple-lane roundabout you may need to cross into the left-hand lane. Make sure you follow the **OSM/PSL** routine. Signal to exit (left) after you have passed the previous exit.

Using roundabouts

See also

For more information on roundabouts, see the video 'Using roundabouts' on the RSA website. To locate the video, type **roundabouts** in the Search box on the home page and then click on **Search**.

My commitment: 16

I can safely negotiate all types of road junction – including left and right turns (from major to minor and from minor to major roads), slip roads, junctions with traffic lights, and roundabouts.

Signed (Learner)

Controlling your speed

The *Rules of the Road* sets out the maximum speed at which you may travel on different types of road. These are maximum speeds: they are not target speeds that you should try to reach.

Roads in built-up areas, such as cities and towns.

Non-national roads (regional and local roads which are signposted with white signs and have an R or L before their number).

National roads (primary and secondary) (green signs - N numbers).

Motorways (blue signs - M numbers).

In addition to the general rules that apply, there are local variations indicated by signs posted along the roadside. These can be temporary (for example, where there are road works), or permanent (at places where the local authority has imposed a speed limit for safety reasons – for example, near a school).

Within the speed limits, travel at a speed that you are comfortable with, and don't feel pressured by other road users into going faster than you want to. You should, however, try to keep up with the general flow of traffic within speed limits and not travel so slowly that you could become a hazard for other road users.

Your ADI will advise you about maintaining a speed that is appropriate to the conditions and the traffic you are riding in.

Riding at an even, moderate speed

On the open road, ride at an even speed – don't speed up and slow down for no reason, and avoid having to brake suddenly in the normal course of riding.

Moderate your speed in bad weather conditions, or if there are a lot of pedestrians around, or if the road is very narrow.

Change your speed evenly and smoothly, both when you are accelerating and when you are slowing down – this is safer and uses less fuel.

Keep your speed in check – check your speedometer regularly. You might be travelling faster than you think – especially if you are in a town or suburb immediately after you have been riding on a higher speed road (such as a dual carriageway).

Slowing down at bends

Dangerous bends and corners are generally indicated by warning signs at the side of the road. These indicate the direction and sharpness of the turn.

As you approach a bend, you need to judge your own speed and decide whether or not you need to slow down. Braking is much safer when the bike is in the upright position. When the bike is leaning around a bend, braking can affect the stability of the bike and cause a skid. So, reduce your speed in advance of the bend (and change down a gear if necessary). Accelerate gently out of the bend.

Where the road marking SLOW is shown before a bend, reduce your speed.

My commitment: 17

I understand the importance of riding at speeds appropriate to the road conditions, and I will always ride within the legal speed limits.

Signed (Learner)

Signalling your intentions

Communicating and cooperating with other road users is very important to road safety. You need to let other road users know what you are about to do, and you need to correctly interpret signals that other drivers give you. The most important signals you can use are your indicators, but in different circumstances, you can also use your horn or hand signals. Your ADI will advise you about what is appropriate.

When to use your indicators

You must use your indicator to signal when you intend to change direction, such as when you intend to:

○ Move off or stop;

○ Turn (left or right) onto another road;

○ Change lanes;

○ Turn off a roundabout;

○ Overtake a slower-moving vehicle;

○ Move around an obstruction – for example, a bus that has pulled in at a bus stop; or

○ Pull into or out of a parking space.

Turn the indicator on early to let other road users know what you are going to do and allow them to respond appropriately, but not so early that you are likely to cause confusion.

Make the turn when it is safe to do so – just turning on the indicator does not give you the automatic right to turn. For example, when turning right off a main road, you must yield to traffic coming against you; and when turning, you must yield to pedestrians already crossing the road.

There may be situations where you have to be especially careful about when to give the signal – for example, if there are two left turns, one very closely after the other.

Make sure to turn off your indicator after you complete the manoeuvre.

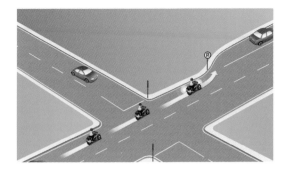

Signalling at the right time. The bike has cleared the junction before signalling to turn into the parking space.

Using your horn

Your motorcycle's horn is an important safety feature that you can use to warn other road users who you think might not have seen you. Don't use your horn aggressively.

Brake lights

Every time you apply the brake, your brake lights come on. This gives vehicles behind you a signal that you are slowing down.

My commitment: 18
I know when and how to signal my intentions to other road users – including when to use direction indicators and the horn.
Signed (Learner)

Interpreting other road users' intentions

Becoming a safe and responsible motorcyclist means that you have to be able to interpret other road users' signals and sometimes second-guess what other people are going to do. Direction indicators are the easiest to interpret, but you will learn to interpret a wide range of signals, intended and unintended, that other road users give. Using a signal does not give you a right of way.

Drivers and motorcyclists signal their intentions clearly when they turn on their indicators or apply their brakes. But they also signal their intentions in more subtle ways – for example, by changing speed, by changing lane or changing direction, by pulling in to the side of the road, and so on. However, not every driver or motorcyclist will signal their intentions clearly.

'This driver looks as if she is about to reverse.'

You need to develop:

○ **Skills of observation** ... so that you notice subtle changes in other road users' behaviour; and

○ **Skills of interpretation** ... so that you can correctly interpret what these changes in behaviour mean.

Practice tip

Misleading signals

Don't always trust other road users to do the right thing or to do what they say they're going to do – being 'in the right' might not be much consolation if you have a collision. One common mistake that some motorists and motorcyclists make is not to turn off the indicator after a turn.

My commitment: 19

I can usually interpret other road users' intentions – from the signals they give and also from subtle changes in their behaviour.

Signed (Learner)

Overtaking

The ability to overtake slower-moving vehicles safely is one you need to develop. You should always be extremely careful when overtaking on the open road and should always ask yourself these questions:

Is it necessary?	If you are going to turn off the road a few hundred metres further on, or if the vehicle ahead is travelling only slightly slower than you want to go, the answer is probably 'no'.
Is it legal?	In particular, check the road markings. Never cross a continuous white line (except in an emergency). And don't overtake if you would need to exceed the speed limit to do so.
Is it safe?	Make sure the road ahead is clear and you have enough room to overtake and return to your own side of the road. Overtaking a long vehicle while going uphill might take longer than you think. If in doubt, don't do it. Also make sure that the location is safe – for example, don't overtake at a humpbacked bridge, or at a turn or dip in the road.

To overtake safely, you need to develop very good judgement of the speed of your motorcycle, that of the vehicle you want to overtake and that of other vehicles – including those coming against you. Don't ever 'take a chance'.

Overtaking on the left

You must normally overtake on the right. However, you are allowed to overtake on the left in the following situations:

- You want to go straight ahead, when the driver in front of you has moved out and signalled that they intend to turn right.
- You have signalled that you intend to turn left.
- Traffic in both lanes is moving slowly and traffic in the left-hand lane is moving more quickly than the traffic in the right-hand lane.

Be aware, however, that other road users might not be expecting to be overtaken on the left, and you might startle them.

My commitment: 20
I am able to overtake slower-moving vehicles.
However, I will do so only when it is necessary, legal and safe.
Signed (Learner)

Balance and control manoeuvres

During a course of Initial Basic Training, your ADI will coach you in how to perform balance and control manoeuvres such as U-turns, figures-of-eight and slaloms. Practising these manoeuvres will help you to develop the control, balance and coordination that will help you to become a better motorcyclist, and you will also have more confidence in your own ability to manoeuvre the bike in tight spaces. You will be asked to perform one of these manoeuvres during your practical test.

Practice tip

In all of these manoeuvres, keep the following points in mind as you practise:

- Maintain your balance without putting your feet on the ground;
- Try to achieve smooth, easy action and good coordination of the clutch, throttle and the rear brake;
- Keep your head up and look in the direction you want to go; and
- Use your weight and the weight of the bike to achieve more fluid steering.

Figure-of-eight

To perform a figure-of-eight, you ride at slow speed in the shape of the figure 8 in a confined space. This requires precise control of the clutch, throttle and brakes; and you need to be able to change from left to right 'lock'.

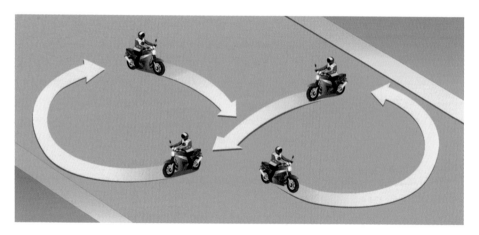

U-turns

Sometimes you have to change the direction you're going in and turn back. You need to learn how to do this safely and competently.

Practise turning around in a safe traffic-free environment and then on quiet side roads before you have to do it on a main road.

 Don't attempt a U-turn where this is not permitted.

Before you do a U-turn, make sure the place you have chosen is safe and legal, and that you are not on a one-way street – follow the **OSM/PSL** routine. The slower you go, the smaller the turning circle that you need.

Slalom

Practising a slalom is a good way of learning how to negotiate in and out of tight situations. Shift the weight of the bike from side to side as you steer, and avoid steering too sharply.

My commitment: 21

I have practised advanced steering manoeuvres, and am confident that I have developed the control, balance and coordination necessary to control the motorcycle.

Signed (Learner)

Stopping in an emergency

In your general on-road practice, you need to always expect the unexpected. You literally don't know what's around the next bend, but you can avoid some dangerous situations by developing your observation skills and learning to anticipate danger. Even the best and safest motorcyclists, however, will have to make emergency stops from time to time. The quicker you respond to a potential emergency, the more likely you are to avert it. So, keep alert and be ready.

In an emergency situation, your aim is to stop as quickly as possible while keeping control of the bike:

- If you brake too strongly, the bike may skid out of control; and
- If you don't brake strongly enough, you won't stop in time.

Keep both hands on the handlebars while you are braking – all your concentration must go on controlling the bike and bringing it safely to a stop.

Practice tip

Emergency braking is one of the topics covered in your Initial Basic Training.

Under the supervision of your ADI, you can practise in a safe and traffic-free environment. This will help you understand the different forces at play and how weight is transferred when you are braking.

Your stopping distance also depends on the quality of your tyres, the road surface and whether it is dry or wet.

My commitment: 22

I will always ride my motorcycle in a safe and responsible manner, and I will try to anticipate dangerous situations before they arise.

I have practised stopping very quickly as I may need to do this in a real emergency.

Signed (Learner)

Riding on motorways

Only motorcyclists with a full licence are permitted to ride on motorways, so while you are still a learner you may not practise on a motorway.

You can, however, begin to learn about motorways by accompanying an experienced driver (in a car) on a motorway journey. You can observe the points that make motorways different from or more challenging than ordinary roads.

Motorway riding

The *Rules of the Road* gives comprehensive guidance on motorway driving and also shows examples of the advance signs and warning signs you will meet on the motorway. Revise these sections before your observation journey.

Dealing with fast-moving traffic

Motorways are designed so that traffic can move very freely and at higher speeds than on ordinary national routes (N-roads). Riding a motorcycle in fast-moving traffic in multiple lanes requires total concentration and keen observation. Even the slightest distraction can have very serious consequences.

Motorways can also be very monotonous and tiring, and tiredness is a major contributor to motorway collisions. Make sure you are well-rested before starting a long motorway journey. If you feel tired, take a break in a safe place off the motorway.

Knowing where you're going

When you are intending to travel on a motorway you need to plan your route much more carefully than you would on N-roads or regional roads – you can't stop and ask for directions, and you can't do a U-turn.

Getting onto the motorway

Finding your way around motorway junctions can be quite confusing and you can easily lose your bearings. On slip roads, in particular, you might have the feeling that you are going around in circles. For that reason you need to study the direction signs much more carefully than on N-roads, and you need to know the outline of your route in advance.

Which exit to take

When you are on the motorway, you need to know which exit to take and you need to get into the correct lane well in advance of the exit. For example, if you are travelling from Portlaoise to Kildare, you leave the M7 at junction 13. Advance information is posted at 2-kilometre and 1-kilometre points ahead of each junction.

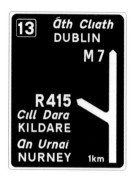

This advance direction shows that the turn-off for Kildare and Nurney is 1 kilometre away.

Motorway end points

You also need to know the end point of the motorway you are travelling on. For example, if you are travelling from Thurles to Clonmel, you join the M8 near Cashel and follow the signs for Cork (not Dublin). Clonmel will not be signposted until you get closer to the exit that leads to Clonmel – junction 10, near Cahir.

Points of the compass

In some cases, directions are indicated as points of the compass, so you need to know which direction you are going in.

- For example, if you are travelling from Finglas to Drogheda, you join the M50 at Finglas by taking the access road marked M50-**Northbound** Dublin Port.

- Similarly, if you are travelling from Finglas to Bray, you join the M50 at Finglas and by taking the access road marked M50-**Southbound** Dún Laoghaire.

See also

Getting help with route planning

The Ordnance Survey publishes a range of maps and atlases, including the *Official Road Atlas Ireland*. There are also many online resources that you can use to help you find the best route to where you want to go.

My commitment: 23

I have a full motorcycle driving licence, have practised motorway riding and understand the challenges that it presents; and in particular, I appreciate the concentration required to ride for prolonged periods at high speed. I understand the importance of good route planning in advance of beginning a motorway journey.

Signed (Learner)

5. Dealing with more challenging conditions

In this chapter

By this stage you have developed your skills as a motorcyclist and have built up a lot of experience on the road. You have completed your Initial Basic Training with an ADI, you are comfortable in the saddle and are familiar with most of the situations you are likely to face in the normal course of riding.

This chapter moves on to look at some of the more challenging conditions that you will face on the road. Most of these are conditions that you will need to learn about at first hand – including riding in heavy traffic, riding at night and in bad weather. Other conditions, such as heavy snow or ice, are not that common in Ireland, but you need to know how to handle them when you come across them.

In the course of your practice journeys, you will sometimes come across challenging conditions without warning. For example, there might be a sudden downpour or you might find yourself in traffic coming from a sporting event you didn't know about. In such conditions, the important thing is to keep up the good habits you have already learnt, and just apply them to the changed circumstances. The key skills of observation, judgement, planning and reaction still apply.

Combinations of challenging conditions

Challenging conditions can become even more difficult when they come in combination – for example, riding at night in very heavy rain on a very busy national road. Usually, when conditions are challenging, you will need to reduce your speed and to be even more careful to observe what's going on.

Dealing with hazards

A hazard is anything that means you might have to change the position, speed, or direction of your motorcycle. For example, a road feature such as a sharp bend could be a hazard, and so could the actions of other road users.

As you build up experience of road and traffic conditions, you will become better at scanning the road ahead to anticipate and react to the different kinds of hazard that you meet. This will help you to further develop the essential skills of observation, judgement, planning and reaction. The rest of this chapter deals with challenging conditions where you need to make use of these skills.

Riding in heavy traffic

Riding in heavy traffic can be a challenging experience. You have to go a lot more slowly than normal, it takes longer to get to where you're going, and you use up a lot more fuel stopping and starting and riding in low gears. Also, traffic conditions are unpredictable, which can lead to unexpected delays and frustration. You need to learn how to anticipate and react to changing conditions in traffic situations.

Why is riding in heavy traffic challenging?

In heavy traffic you are likely to be riding at low speeds, and stopping and starting quite a lot – this brings with it a number of challenges. Keep in mind that:

O Your control of the brake, clutch and throttle needs to be very good – your left hand will spend quite a lot of time on the clutch and your right foot will hover just above the rear brake pedal;

O You could be 'surrounded' in a middle lane with vehicles, perhaps trucks or buses, on both sides; and

O Changing lane can be very difficult – you are relying on the courtesy of drivers in other lanes to let you change.

Do not 'filter' or weave through lanes of stopped or slow-moving traffic, as this can be dangerous.

Other road users: risks and intimidation

In heavy, slow-moving traffic, some drivers and motorcyclists get frustrated – they're late for work or for an appointment, or they just want to get home. Research shows that the highest number of traffic collisions happen during the evening rush, between 4 and 6 o'clock, when traffic is at its heaviest.

The biggest challenges you are likely to face in heavy traffic come from other road users:

- Some car drivers may take unnecessary risks, such as changing lanes very suddenly or taking a chance at a level crossing. You need to stay very alert to such behaviour.

- Other drivers may try to intimidate you in various ways – for example by sounding the horn when you stop at an amber light; or when you correctly wait until a box junction is clear before you cross it.

My commitment: 24
I have practised riding in heavy traffic. I am confident that I can control the motorcycle, remain patient, and deal with the frustrations of being stuck in traffic.

Signed (Learner)

Night-time riding

Why is riding at night challenging?

Your skills of observation depend on what you can actually see, but they also depend on your perception – that is, your awareness and judgement of other factors. For example, you need to be able to judge how far away or how near things are. Also, you need to be able to estimate the speed of other vehicles relative to your own speed, and you need to be aware of differences in colour and light. Your observation skills also depend on your peripheral vision – that is what you can see out of the corner of your eye. At night, you can see less and therefore you have much less information to help you decide what action to take. This is especially the case when you're riding on unlit rural roads.

Tiredness and other factors at night

You're more likely to be tired at night, and this will affect your observation skills as well as your reaction times. There are other factors that can make riding at night challenging. Remember that:

○ Traffic is generally much lighter at night, and some car drivers and motorcyclists are tempted to drive faster than they ought to.

○ At night you are much more likely to be sharing the road with people whose behaviour is affected by alcohol or tiredness.

○ You can be dazzled by both oncoming and following drivers who don't dip their main headlights. Even if you're not dazzled, going against a steady stream of cars with dipped lights can be very tiring and a strain on your eyes, which are constantly adjusting between darkness and very bright light.

Night-time riding

The *Rules of the Road gives* detailed advice on riding at night.

Some tips for riding safely at night

About a third of all serious road collisions take place at night. This is a very high proportion considering the relatively low volumes of traffic on the roads at night. For that reason alone, you need to pay extra attention when riding at night, particularly while you are learning.

○ You don't necessarily have to go slower at night; but you do need take into consideration that your perception of possible hazards is limited. If you don't think you could safely bring the bike to a stop within the distance of what you can see with your dipped headlight, then you're travelling too fast – slow down!

○ Riding at night presents special challenges, especially in unlit places. Headlights from oncoming cars can really affect your night vision. Slow down and maintain a safe course, and avoid looking directly into the headlights of oncoming vehicles. It might take your eyes some time to adjust to different light conditions.

○ Think of other road users and dip your headlight when you see the lights of an oncoming vehicle. You should also dip your light when you are following another vehicle, to avoid causing mirror dazzle. If you suspect that your light is not correctly aligned (in other words that even with dipped headlight you are still dazzling oncoming vehicles), have it checked by a mechanic.

○ Turn on your lights at dusk when daylight begins to fade – don't wait for total darkness to fall. This will help other road users to see you.

- Be seen: wear reflective clothing to make it easier for other road users to see you.
- Make sure that all lights and reflectors are clean and in working order at all times, especially at night.
- Poor night vision can be a serious traffic hazard. Symptoms include difficulty seeing when riding in the evening or at night, poor vision in reduced light, and feeling that the eyes take longer to 'adjust' to seeing in the dark. If you have concerns about your night vision, seek medical advice.
- Use auxiliary lights (extra lights such as fog lights and spot lights) only when appropriate and legal.
- Don't use a tinted visor at night. Also, don't use a scratched visor, as this could distort your vision at night, especially in wet conditions.

Driving in rural areas at night

When riding at night in unlit rural areas, use full beam headlight to give yourself the best view of the road ahead. Even with full beam turned on, you should ride within the limits of what you could see if you were riding with dipped headlight – as you may need to dip your light suddenly. Make sure to dip your headlight when:

- You meet an oncoming vehicle or other road user; and
- You are closely following another vehicle – your full beams reflecting in the mirror of the vehicle in front can be very dazzling.

Overtaking at night

Avoid overtaking at night unless it's necessary. Take extra care when doing so, as reduced visibility makes it more difficult to judge speed and distance.

Practice tip | The purpose of your lights is to help you see and be seen – they're not just for when it's dark, but for any situation where visibility is poor. Turning on your lights does not shorten the life of your battery. Many experienced motorcyclists and drivers turn on their dipped headlight or daytime running lights during daylight hours.

My commitment: 25

I have practised riding my motorcycle at night on a variety of different roads, urban and rural. I understand the particular dangers of riding at night and will always ride with consideration for other road users.

Signed (Learner)

Riding in conditions of poor visibility

Any kind of weather that makes it more difficult for you to see what's happening on the road (and makes it more difficult for other road users to see you) presents particular riding challenges, especially for the learner.

Riding in heavy rain

In very heavy rain (or falling snow, hailstones or sleet) your visibility is reduced a good deal. You're looking at the road through a continuous sheet of rain, your visor is covered in droplets, and the cold air is likely to cause your visor to mist up on the inside. You also have to cope with splashes or spray from passing cars, heavy goods vehicles and buses. At night-time the wet road surface reflects the lights of oncoming cars and causes glare.

In addition to poor visibility, you need to be aware that a wet road surface does not give your tyres the same level of grip as a dry surface. The road might be particularly slippery when it gets wet after a long spell of dry weather.

What is aquaplaning?

Aquaplaning happens when you are riding on a wet road. The tyre treads fill with water and are unable to disperse it to the side, so that your tyres are riding on a thin film of water and are not in direct contact with the road surface.

If the bike aquaplanes, the steering will seem very 'loose'. Stay calm, ease off the throttle to slow down, but avoid braking if possible. At a slower speed the water will be dispersed and the tyres will regain their grip on the road surface.

Moderate your speed during heavy rain or where water is building up on the road surface. This will help to avoid aquaplaning

What can you do?

There are a number of things you can do to help make riding safer in heavy rain (or falling snow, hailstones or sleet):

- Turn on your headlight (dipped) so that other road users can see you more easily.
- Slow down and stay further back from the vehicle in front of you, especially if this is a bus or a heavy goods vehicle that is making a lot of spray. You still need to keep up with the general flow of traffic, but bear in mind that your stopping distance is much greater on wet, greasy roads.
- Be considerate in how you treat other road users in very heavy rain. Remember that:
  - A pedestrian with an umbrella facing into the wind might not see traffic, and the noise of the rain might also drown out the sound of traffic.

- When approaching pedestrians and cyclists you should be careful not to splash them as you pass. Take into account that bicycle brakes don't work very well when wet.
- Motorcyclists also have very limited vision in heavy rain. So if you're following another motorcycle, increase the gap to allow for the greater stopping distances required.

O Brake earlier and more gently than you normally would.

Localised flooding?

When you have ridden through a large puddle or area of localised flooding, your brakes may become less effective. In this case, test your brakes to ensure that they have not been affected by the water – check in your mirrors before you do this.

If they have been affected, it is more than likely that this is just temporary. When it is safe to do so, gently apply both brakes to make sure they are dry and working as normal.

Riding in fog

Fog is one of the most dangerous weather conditions for all kinds of transport. In dense fog, airports close down and ships stay in port. On the roads, fog can (depending on how dense it is) range from being a minor nuisance to being a serious danger.

What can you do?

Riding a motorcycle in dense fog is not recommended, and you should not travel in foggy conditions unless you really have to. Fog, however, is often quite localised and can come down suddenly without warning. You need to be prepared for it and to know how to behave if you do find yourself riding in fog. There are a number of things you can do to help make riding in fog safer:

O Make sure to stay a safe distance from the vehicle in front of you, and be satisfied at all times that you can stop within the distance that you can see to be clear.

O Drive at a steady, slow speed. Fog is usually patchy and you will pass through areas where visibility varies. Don't be tempted to speed up through the good patches, as you might find yourself all of a sudden in another dense patch. (Most motorway pile-ups happen when vehicles are driving too fast and too close together.)

O Make sure that other road users can see you. Turn on your headlight (dipped) and/or fog lights. Don't turn on your main beam headlight, as this just beams into the fog and makes it more difficult to see where you're going. Turn on your rear fog lights if you have them – but remember to turn them off when the fog is gone.

O Stay in the centre of the lane: if you ride too close to the left edge, you might come across a parked vehicle unexpectedly; if you ride too close to the centre of the road, you might be too close to oncoming traffic.

O At junctions, listen for any approaching traffic– you might hear a vehicle coming before you see it.

Facing into a low sun

We usually associate poor visibility with bad weather, but good weather can also cause problems. You can be dazzled when riding into a low sun (particularly in winter). Wear sunglasses or use a tinted visor to shade your eyes.

My commitment: 26

I have practised riding in conditions of poor daytime visibility. I appreciate the importance of seeing and being seen.

Signed (Learner)

Riding in poor on-road conditions

In conditions where the road is covered with snow or ice, or is flooded or has patches of loose gravel, your grip on the road can be much impaired. In these conditions, you are more likely to lose control of your motorcycle, especially at higher speeds.

Snow and ice

Snow and ice can make the road surface very hazardous, and as far as possible you should avoid riding in snow or on icy roads or if these are forecast. If you're not sure, listen to traffic reports and weather forecasts and warnings from the Road Safety Authority.

As with fog, snow and icy conditions can arrive quite suddenly, and you might find yourself riding in snow or ice without expecting to.

Fresh snow

Freshly fallen snow is not as slippery on the road as ice or compacted snow. However, you should reduce your speed and keep a good distance from the vehicle in front of you.

Be aware, however, that fresh snow will cover the road markings and catseyes, including those that mark the edge and the middle of the road. If you are the first vehicle to ride on the fresh snow, you might have difficulty knowing where you are on the road. This will be less of a problem in urban areas where roadside buildings and street furniture will guide you and on busier roads where you can follow the tyre tracks of vehicles that have gone before you.

You should also watch out for roadside warning signs that might become covered with snow and become more difficult to read. STOP and YIELD signs have distinctive shapes (octagonal and triangular respectively) for that reason.

Compacted snow and ice

Compacted snow that has frozen overnight is particularly treacherous and as it thaws it becomes even more slippery and dangerous. In such conditions, some roads become impassable – for example those with steep hills or with humpbacked bridges. Even where the road has been gritted and salted by the local authority, you need to proceed with extreme caution.

Riding through the thaw

As weather conditions improve after a period of snow and frost, it's easy to become complacent, but there are a number of things you should look out for:

- There will be sheltered areas with patches of melting ice that are still very slippery – for example, at bends in the road with overhanging bushes.
- There is a risk of skidding on loose grit spread by the local authorities.
- Melting snow and ice may lead to localised flooding.
- The road surface might have been damaged by snow and ice, so you need to be on the lookout for potholes and other hazards.
- Where there is a build-up of slush and ice at the sides of the road, you may have to ride closer to the centre of the road than usual.

Snow and ice: general advice

- Avoid riding in snowy or icy conditions unless you have to.
- Make sure your tyres have at least the minimum legal tread depth (1mm) and are correctly inflated.
- On icy roads, your stopping distance can be up to ten times what it is normally, and it can be very difficult to control the bike as you brake. For that reason, you need to:
  - Slow down;
  - Keep your distance from the vehicle in front; and
  - Make sure that all your manoeuvres are smooth and gentle: brake gently and accelerate very gently.
- If visibility is poor, turn on your dipped headlight.
- Keep yourself informed about road conditions in times of bad weather – see the RSA website for advice, and listen to radio traffic and weather updates.

Black ice

Black ice is an almost invisible, thin coating of ice on the road surface. Because it is hard to see it is particularly dangerous. When the temperature drops close to freezing you can expect to find black ice – particularly in sheltered or shaded areas of the roadway, under trees or beside high walls. Sometimes it can look like a sheet of water or as if the road is wet.

Avoiding skids

The most common causes of skids are going too fast for the on-road conditions, or jerky braking, gear changing or steering. You can reduce the likelihood of skidding by riding smoothly at an appropriate speed, and by keeping your distance from the vehicle in front. Be particularly careful when approaching bends, especially those on a downslope.

Don't rely on your ABS to prevent you from skidding – it won't always do so.

My commitment: 27

I appreciate the dangers of riding a motorcycle in snow and ice, and I will not make any unnecessary journeys in such conditions.

When I do ride in snow and ice I will ride more slowly, leave more room ahead, and accelerate and brake smoothly and gently.

Signed (Learner)

Riding in high winds

Riding a motorcycle in high winds can be a very challenging experience. With only two wheels on the ground, you don't have as much stability as a car, and you can easily be blown off course by a sudden gust of wind, especially a crosswind.

Be particularly alert to crosswinds on exposed stretches of road, on elevated bridges, on the crests of hills, at gateways, and whenever you see the Crosswinds alert sign. In windy conditions, you need to be alert when you change direction – for example, as you round bends on a twisty road, or when you turn onto a different road.

Poor road surface conditions

The quality of the road surface plays a huge role in the experience of riding a motorcycle. Riding on just two wheels, you need to be constantly on the look-out for irregularities and other problems with the road surface. These can include the following:

- Loose chippings;
- Oil spills;
- Rail tracks (at level crossings);
- Manhole covers;
- Mud or farm waste (in rural areas);
- Tram tracks;
- Hot tar;
- Potholes;
- Road markings;
- Smooth road surface markings;
- Temporary plates (at roadworks);
- Debris and litter;
- Wet leaves in autumn; and
- Steep slopes at gutters.

Dealing with road works and other obstructions

The National Roads Authority and local authorities around the country are continually working to provide a safe and efficient road network and to maintain the quality of road surfaces. Roadworks can vary – they could be major jobs or smaller works, and include the construction of new roads, emergency repairs, routine maintenance of fences and barriers, trimming hedgerows, clearing litter, cutting grass verges, and so on.

When you come across roadworks of any kind, you need to proceed with extra care, for your own safety and that of other road users and of the road workers.

Roadworks challenges

Roadworks present challenges to all road users. These include: :

- Detours and different traffic patterns
- Different lane markers and traffic cones
- Contraflows on motorways and dual carriageways
- Stop–Go systems or temporary traffic lights
- Loose chippings
- Unfinished or very uneven road surfaces
- Narrower lanes than usual and restricted shoulder areas
- Large, slow-moving works vehicles on the road

Warning signs

The *Rules of the Road* lists the warning signs relating to road works.
These signs give warnings, advice and instructions relating to road works,
including speed restrictions, detours and road surface conditions. Make
sure that you understand what all of these warning signs mean.

Staying safe at roadworks

Follow these easy guidelines to help maintain safety at road works:

O Slow down and obey the temporary speed limits posted.

O Obey all the signs, temporary traffic lights and any instructions given to you by flagmen and
   other road workers.

O Keep a safe distance from the vehicle in front.

O Follow the lane markers and cones (where present).

O Be alert to the movements of road workers and of works traffic.

My commitment: 28

I will always ride through road works with care and consideration; and I will obey the warning
signs and any instructions the road workers give me.

Signed (Learner)

Town and country: challenges of urban and rural riding

Town and country riding each presents very different kinds of challenges to the motorcyclist. While you are learning to ride, your practice journeys should cover both.

Town and city challenges using a motorcycle

Riding in towns and cities presents you with a variety of difficult situations, often in very quick succession. By this stage in your learning progress you might be reasonably comfortable with complex junctions, multi-lane roundabouts and one-way systems. However, in towns and cities you will come across these challenges much more often, especially in heavy traffic. Hazards you need to be particularly careful about while riding in towns and cities include:

- Obstructions caused by goods vehicles making deliveries;
- Buses pulling in and out at bus stops;
- Cars parked on the side of the street – be careful of doors opening unexpectedly or of children running out from between parked cars;
- More vulnerable road users to consider – including pedestrians and cyclists; and
- Stop-start riding – as the distance between junctions can be quite short.

Urban speed limit

The general speed limit for built-up areas is 50km/h (this might be different for some areas).

Because of all the hazards in the urban environment it is particularly important for motorcyclists to have enough time to react, and you should never exceed the 50km/h limit.

My commitment: 29

I have practised riding on urban streets and understand the particular hazards I am likely to come across there. I will always ride within the urban speed limit.

Signed (Learner)

Rural challenges

On country roads you are more likely to meet slow-moving vehicles, such as tractors and other agricultural vehicles. Don't try to overtake them unless you have a clear view of the road ahead and the road is wide enough to overtake safely. Be patient: they are probably travelling only a very short distance.

Many narrow country roads do not have central road markings and allow very little room for two vehicles to pass. You are also more likely to meet livestock on country roads. Be prepared to slow down or stop and don't do anything to frighten the animals.

Visibility

High hedges and the winding nature of country roads can impair visibility – blind corners, sharp bends and dips in the road can be particularly dangerous. You should always adjust your speed to suit the road you are driving on and you must never exceed the speed limit. In many cases, a safe speed might be much less than the stated speed limit for the road. You need to be able to stop the bike in the road space that you can see – if you can't, you're going too fast.

Road surface

Local authorities give priority to maintaining roads with heavier traffic, so country roads with less traffic might not have the same surface quality. Also, on country roads watch out for loose gravel, mud and things like fallen leaves – all of these can make the surface slippery, especially after rain.

My commitment: 30

I have practised riding on country roads and I understand that visibility might be poor and that the road surfaces might be more uneven than on urban or national roads. While riding on country roads I will be considerate to the needs of farmers and other country dwellers and their animals.

Signed (Learner)

Carrying a passenger

When you carry a pillion passenger, you are taking responsibility for that person's safety and comfort. Don't carry a passenger unless you are totally satisfied that it is safe and legal to do so.

Are you licensed and insured?

You may carry a pillion passenger only if you have a full licence for the category of motorcycle you're riding. You must also have appropriate insurance cover.

Is your bike suitable?

Your motorcycle must be equipped with a proper pillion saddle and passenger footrests. The passenger must be tall enough to reach the footrests comfortably.

In addition, to cater for the additional weight on the bike, there are a number of checks you need to make. For some of these you will need to check the manufacturer's instructions or the bike's maintenance manual. You may have to, for example:

O Inflate the tyres to a higher pressure;

O Increase the pressure in the rear shock absorber – this will ensure that the rear tyre remains well clear of the mudguard;

O Adjust the dipped headlight beam – with extra weight on the rear of the bike, the beam will be aimed higher, so you need to lower it so that you don't dazzle oncoming vehicles; and

O Adjust your mirrors.

Is your passenger ready?

Your passenger must wear a correctly-fitting helmet and appropriate protective clothing. For night riding, your passenger should have reflective clothing. (See page 21 for more details about protective clothing.)

If your passenger doesn't have much experience of being on a motorcycle you will need to tell them what to expect before setting out. For a first-time passenger, riding pillion can be quite a frightening experience, especially when you lean around corners. Make sure that the passenger agrees to:

O Sit properly on the pillion saddle with both feet on the footrests;

O Hold on to your waist or onto the passenger handle(s) (where fitted);

O Lean with you as you go around corners and bends; and

O Not make any movements that could destabilise the bike in motion.

Are you ready?

Riding with a pillion passenger changes much of the 'feel' of the bike, mostly because of the extra weight, but also because the centre of gravity of the bike is now further back. Here are some points you need to think about:

- Acceleration will be slower, so you might need to give yourself more room when overtaking;
- Braking will take longer, so you should leave more space between you and the vehicle in front;
- When you brake (especially if you do so suddenly), your passenger will be pushed into your back;
- There will be less 'ground clearance' or space between the body of the motorcycle and the road, and this could be a problem on rough or bumpy road surfaces. (This will be less of a problem if you increase the pressure in the rear shock absorber.)
- The bike will be more difficult to balance, especially at lower speeds and as you go around bends and corners; and
- With two people on board, you present a much bigger 'sail' for crosswinds.

Try it yourself

Practice tip

You will understand what's involved in being a pillion passenger if you have done it yourself. Ask your ADI to let you ride as a pillion passenger to get an idea of what it's like.

My commitment: 31

I accept that I am fully responsible for the safety and comfort of any pillion passenger I take with me on the road.

I will take a passenger only when I am satisfied that it is safe and legal to do so.

I understand that the motorcycle will handle differently with a passenger on board.

Signed (Learner)

Carrying luggage

You can use a variety of fittings to carry luggage and other items on your motorcycle. Among the more popular are:

Panniers	Make sure to load each side evenly.
Top box	Don't overload them, as this could make the bike unstable.
Luggage rack	Make sure all luggage items are securely tied down or fastened to the rack.
Tank bag	This should never interfere with your steering.

Some of the points that you have to consider before you take on a pillion passenger also apply in relation to carrying luggage. In particular, if you place a lot of weight on the rear of the bike, then you may need to inflate the tyres to a higher pressure, adjust the rear shock absorber, and check the headlight beam.

When you are on the road, you also need to allow for greater stopping distances and slower acceleration.

6. Sharing the road

In this chapter

As you probably know by now, the basic skills of riding a motorcycle are generally not that difficult to master. With the help of your ADI and a well-planned schedule of riding practice, you can be competent in all the major skills in a matter of weeks. By this stage, you've probably also come to understand the importance of sharing the road responsibly with other people. Learning to do that is much more difficult than learning to control the bike, and you need to:

- Be in good physical and mental condition to ride safely and competently;
- Stay calm even if other road users are behaving badly, and do not allow your own emotions to get the better of you;
- Avoid distractions while you are on the road, but learn to deal with those that do arise;
- Behave with consideration and courtesy to other road users, including pedestrians, cyclists, motorists and drivers of larger vehicles;
- Consider how you can reduce the impact of your road use on the environment; and
- Know what to do if you arrive at the scene of a collision.

Staying healthy

Medical conditions

Some medical conditions can have an effect on how well you ride your motorcycle. Even a bad cold or a simple viral infection can slow down your reaction time and lower your concentration levels. If you are currently being treated for any medical condition, ask your doctor if it is safe for you to ride.

Facts about alcohol

- Driver alcohol consumption is a factor in about a quarter of all fatal collisions in Ireland.
- Across Europe, alcohol or drugs are a factor in almost a quarter of all collisions, leading to about 10,000 deaths a year.

The effects of alcohol: never ever drink and drive/ride

Riding a motorcycle while under the influence of alcohol puts you at a much greater risk of being involved in a collision. Collisions caused by drink-driving or riding are usually preventable. Never, ever drink and drive/ride. It's not worth the risk, either to yourself or other road users. The legal limits for alcohol consumption apply equally to motorists and to motorcyclists. As a motorcyclist, you are likely to come off much worse than a car-driver in the event of a collision – remember just how vulnerable you are.

Alcohol slows down your nervous system and causes you to function less effectively in many different ways; in summary, alcohol:

O Impairs your vision and reduces your 'field of vision' – in particular your peripheral vision (what you see out of the corner of your eye);

O Impairs your perception – your ability to judge how far away objects are, including cars and other vehicles;

O Makes it more difficult for you to coordinate the various tasks that riding a motorcycle involves – balancing, steering, braking, observing road signs, and so on;

O Dulls your reflexes so that you are no longer able to react as quickly in dangerous situations. In other words, your reaction time is much longer and your physical movements (for example, pulling on the brake) are much slower; and

O Causes loss of judgement, gives you false confidence and lack of inhibition in relation to speed, which in turn lead to 'taking a chance'.

The effects of other drugs

Drugs (legal and illegal) other than alcohol can impair your ability and change the way you ride. For example, drugs such as depressants dull your reactions, while stimulants heighten your senses and can make you overreact.

O Depressants (or downers) have similar effects to alcohol and are particularly dangerous when taken with alcohol. Prescribed depressants include tranquillisers for relief of anxiety and tension.

O Narcotics include some legally prescribed pain-killers and illegal drugs such as heroin and cannabis. Their effects include euphoria (feeling unnaturally happy), giddiness and drowsiness.

O Hallucinogenic drugs lead to nausea and altered states of perception – which is especially dangerous considering how important good perception is to a motorcyclist. This category of drugs includes Ecstasy and LSD.

O Stimulants are used medicinally to increase alertness and to relieve tiredness. They can also cause hyperactivity, aggressiveness and reckless behaviour – all of which impair your ability to ride safely.

If you are taking any kind of medication, prescribed or over-the-counter, ask your doctor or pharmacist to confirm that it's OK to ride a motorcycle.

The effects of tiredness

Fatigue – or tiredness – is one of the main causes of serious road collisions. When you're very tired, you are much less alert, have poorer physical coordination and your reaction times are much longer. Your level of concentration is lower and you find it more difficult to 'read the road' and take in direction signs, warning signs and other information as you go.

You are more likely to become tired when riding on main roads with low traffic volumes (particularly on motorways), where the riding task is monotonous and there is very little stimulation. Other conditions that can lead to tiredness include:

- Riding in traffic jams or very slow-moving traffic;
- Riding in rain or other poor weather conditions – when you need higher levels of concentration;
- Prolonged exposure to the noise and vibration of the motorcycle engine; and
- At night, when you would normally be asleep – in particular, the glare from oncoming headlights can cause eye fatigue.

Avoiding and handling tiredness

The best way to handle tiredness is to avoid it in the first place – in particular, make sure you are well rested in advance of a longer journey. Don't depend on coffee to keep away fatigue. There are some things you can do to avoid and handle tiredness. For instance:

- On longer trips, take a 15-minute break at least once every two hours: get off the bike in a safe location and stretch your legs;
- Make sure you are comfortable on the bike and have good posture; and
- Wear suitable clothing to give you protection against the weather.

My commitment: 32

I will ride a motorcycle only when I am physically and mentally fit to do so.

I will never ever drink and drive/ride.

I will never ever ride a motorcycle while under the influence of drugs (legal or illegal).

Signed (Learner)

Staying calm: showing courtesy

There are so many things that can stress you when you are on the road: heavy traffic, bad weather, waiting at level crossings – all of these can build up frustration and make it difficult to stay calm and focus on arriving safely at your destination. Your own emotional state can also play a big part in how well you ride. If you are worried or upset, angry or depressed, it will probably show in your on-road behaviour. If you need to, take a short break to compose yourself before you get on the bike.

If you're late for an appointment, accept the fact – stop the bike in a safe place and phone ahead to let the person expecting you know that you'll be a little late. You can help to reduce stress by giving yourself enough time to get to your destination without feeling rushed. Don't allow yourself to become impatient, as this can lead to rash behaviour and taking unnecessary risks. Cooperate with other road users and remain courteous and tolerant in your dealings with them, particularly more vulnerable road users such as pedestrians and cyclists.

Annoying actions to avoid

Think about your own riding behaviour. Are there things you do that could annoy other road users? The most common annoying actions (some of which are illegal) include:

- Tailgating – riding too close to the vehicle in front;
- Signalling very late before turning – the vehicles behind might not be able to move around you;
- Not dipping your main headlight when you meet oncoming vehicles;
- Passing on the inside in fast-moving traffic;
- Riding in the outer lane of a dual carriage way or motorway;
- Aggressive use of the horn;
- Weaving in and out of traffic lanes or riding between traffic lanes; and
- Slowing down for no apparent reason or riding significantly below the speed limit for no good reason.

Other road users' behaviour

Some drivers and motorcyclists think of driving or riding as a kind of competitive sport and don't show much consideration for other road users. They will cut inside you, indicate right at the last minute, blare their horn, make aggressive gestures, and so on.

This kind of aggressive behaviour can very easily turn into 'road rage' where people who are normally civil and courteous lose self-control and act very irresponsibly when they feel themselves 'provoked'. Don't allow yourself to be drawn into this kind of 'competition'. Let such drivers or riders go ahead – you will be safer if you are not in their vicinity.

Good drivers and motorcyclists stay patient and courteous at all times and don't respond to provocation– they know that they'll get there just as quickly if they ignore such actions. 'Count to ten' and give yourself time to cool down.

My commitment: 33

I understand the importance of remaining calm, patient and courteous at all times while riding.

I will not allow myself to be 'provoked' by the behaviour of other road users.

Signed (Learner)

Avoiding and dealing with distractions while riding

As you know by now, riding requires you to take in a great deal of information – about other traffic, road conditions, direction and warning signs, and so on. Just dealing with that amount of information is quite enough, and you don't need to add to the load by letting yourself be distracted. A distraction is anything that takes away your concentration while you are on the road; when you are distracted, your reactions will be slower and your judgement will not be as good. It is an offence to ride a motorcycle 'without due care and attention'.

Good drivers and motorcyclists maintain their concentration on the task in hand at all times. They don't allow distractions of any kind to interfere with their number one priority when on the road – to arrive safely at their destination.

Young motorcyclists and peer pressure

Young motorcyclists (particularly young men) are inclined to go faster, pay less attention to the road and are more likely to take chances when they are riding with friends. You need to be aware of these risks and to take responsibility for ensuring that you have a safe journey.

For any young person, learning to ride a motorcycle is a big step towards maturity and you need to show in your on-the-road behaviour that you are now mature enough to resist any peer pressure to go faster or to take risks.

My commitment: 34

I will not do anything that will distract me from my responsibility to ride safely.

I will not respond or react to distractions caused by others.

Signed (Learner)

Dealing with other road users

As a motorcyclist you share the road with car drivers and with many other people as well: cyclists, other motorcyclists, pedestrians, bus and lorry drivers, and sometimes (in rural areas) farm animals. You need to be conscious at all times of the different view of the road that other road users have. And you also need to understand your own responsibilities.

Pedestrians

Pedestrians are the most vulnerable road users, and you should always slow down when riding in an area where there is a lot of pedestrian traffic. You should be especially alert to the safety of small children – for example, when you are near schools. You also need to watch out for elderly people who might not always manage to cross the road before the traffic light changes.

Most rural roads do not have footpaths and pedestrians have to walk on the margin of the road, however unsuitable that might be. For example, in wet weather the road margin might be very soft or muddy underfoot. Slow down if you see pedestrians on either side of the road ahead – don't expect them to move into the ditch.

You can expect to find more pedestrians:

- At and near bus stops;
- At the entrances to railway stations;
- Near schools at opening and closing times;
- Around sports venues;
- Along popular jogging routes;
- Near hospitals; and
- On shopping streets.

Joining a main road

If you are joining a main road from a side road you should give way to pedestrians on the main road who are crossing the side road.

If you are emerging from a private entrance, you should give way to pedestrians on the margin of the road or on the footpath (if there is one).

Vulnerable pedestrians

Watch out for disabled people and other vulnerable road users – including blind and visually impaired pedestrians (with or without guide dogs). Be aware that pedestrians who are deaf or hard of hearing might not hear you coming.

Be careful when passing drivers of powered wheelchairs or other vehicles used by persons with disabilities.

Cyclists

Cyclists are just as entitled to use the road as you are, and you need to pay special attention to them.

- Cyclists can sometimes make sudden movements – for example, to avoid a pothole or some broken glass or other object on the road.
- In bad weather cyclists have less control – they can be blown off balance by strong winds and can find it difficult to see in heavy rain. Also, they can skid very easily in icy conditions.
- At night, cyclists are more difficult to see. Even if they have good lights and reflective clothing, cyclists can get 'lost' in the glare of much stronger car lights.
- When you are passing a cyclist, make sure you leave enough room between your motorcycle and the cyclist. And the faster you are travelling, the more space you should leave. Don't pass a cyclist if the road is too narrow to do so safely. Slow down and wait for a wider stretch of road.

- Check your blind spots for cyclists when you manoeuvre in traffic, especially before you pull out into traffic from a parking space.

- If you are turning left, you should give way to cyclists on your inside who are going straight ahead or turning left – this applies whether or not there is a marked cycle lane. This also applies on roundabouts, where you should not cut across a cyclist to make your exit.

- Do not ride or park on a cycle lane.

- Be particularly careful dealing with children on bicycles, as they might not have very good road sense or control of their bicycles.

- If traffic is moving slowly, cyclists may overtake you on the inside. Always check your external mirrors and your blind spots before turning or pulling into the kerb.

Your fellow motorcyclists

Many of the considerations you need to have for cyclists also apply to your fellow motorcyclists. Like cyclists they are also very vulnerable and can easily become 'hidden' in a blind spot or behind a larger vehicle or other obstacles. Because they travel so much faster than cyclists, dangerous situations can arise much more quickly with motorcyclists.

- Always look out for other motorcyclists when you are emerging from a side road or a private entrance.

- Due to its small size, a motorcycle may seem further away than it actually is, and it may be difficult to judge its speed.

- Keep your distance when travelling behind another motorcycle.

Farm traffic

In rural areas you can expect to meet tractors and other slow-moving agricultural machinery as well as cattle and sheep being herded along the road.

- Be patient if you are behind a tractor and cannot pass – it is probably travelling only a very short distance and will pull into a gateway or a farmyard very shortly.

- Slow down if you meet animals being herded along the road – again, they are probably going only a very short distance. Don't use your horn, as this might frighten the animals.

In more remote areas of open countryside, you might meet sheep on the road or grazing along the roadside. Slow down until you have passed them, as they are easily frightened and not always predictable in their movements.

Larger vehicles

Driving a truck or bus is not an easy job, especially on some of our narrower urban streets and regional roads. The particular problems that truck and bus drivers have are mostly related to the size of their vehicles. As a motorcyclist, you can help to make their job a little easier if you take the following into account.

Blind spots	All vehicles have some blind spots, and the bigger the vehicle, the bigger the blind spots. If you are riding behind a truck and you cannot see the truck's mirror, then the truck driver cannot see you.
	Truck cabs tend to be quite high above the road, so the space immediately in front of the truck at ground level can also be a blind spot.
Turning room	Trucks and buses usually need to swing quite wide to the right before they make a left turn. Do not attempt to pass a truck or bus on the inside when it is turning left – you could end up being caught between the truck and the kerb.
Reversing	Trucks and buses sometimes have to reverse into quite restricted spaces – this is especially true for trucks delivering goods. Don't cross behind a large vehicle while it is reversing.
Bus stops	Passenger buses stop frequently to set down and take on passengers, and you should be careful of pedestrians in the vicinity of bus stops. You should give way to a bus that is signalling its intention to rejoin the stream of traffic.

My commitment: 35

I will treat all other road users with courtesy and respect, particularly more vulnerable road users such as pedestrians, cyclists and other motorcyclists.

Signed (Learner)

Thinking of the environment

The motor industry is making substantial efforts to reduce the environmental damage caused by driving. Modern cars and motorcycles are generally much more efficient in their use of fuel, have lower greenhouse gas emissions, and cause less pollution.

As individual motorcyclists, we can also do quite a lot to reduce our personal carbon footprint and to minimise the impact our road use has on the environment.

Fuel-efficient riding

There are a number of simple steps you can take to make your motorcycling more fuel-efficient, and save you money. Motorcyclists who follow these steps also tend to be safer.

Ride smoothly

For greater fuel efficiency, speed up gradually, slow down gradually and ride smoothly in as high a gear as possible.

- The faster you accelerate the more fuel you use, and there is often very little point in accelerating away from one traffic light only to meet a red light at the next.
- Revving or racing your engine while you wait at traffic lights is simply a waste of fuel.
- Remember to turn off the choke (if fitted) once the engine has warmed up.
- Less stopping and starting is more economical.

Reduce your speed

On main roads and motorways, the faster you go the more fuel you are using. For example, travelling at 120km/h on a motorway you use up to 20% more fuel than travelling at 100km/h; and on a 20km journey, the time saving would be only two minutes. Can you afford to be in such a hurry?

Avoid unnecessary idling

If you're stopping for more than 30 seconds or so (except in traffic), turn off the engine; and never leave your engine on when you are parked.

Service your motorcycle regularly

Service your bike regularly to ensure that you get the best performance and best fuel efficiency. Simple changes such as replacing worn spark plugs and clogged air filters can save fuel consumption by up to ten per cent.

Check your tyre pressure regularly

Check your tyre pressure regularly and make sure that you follow the manufacturer's guidelines for your bike. Under-inflated tyres drag more on the road so your engine has to work harder and uses more fuel. Over-inflating your tyres can be dangerous, as they will then have less grip on the road.

Reduce your load

The greater the weight on your bike, the more fuel the engine uses. Don't carry unnecessary objects around in your panniers, top box or luggage rack.

Ride less and plan ahead

Is your trip really necessary? Could you walk or use public transport? Could you combine a number of trips into one? Is there a better time of day for a particular trip? Would a bike with a smaller engine suit your needs just as well?

Especially in urban areas, a very high percentage of motor journeys are very short; and at certain times of the day and in heavy traffic, it may be much quicker to use an alternative form of transport.

My commitment: 36

I accept that riding a motorcycle has an impact on the environment. I will try to minimise that impact by the way that I use my motorcycle.

Signed (Learner)

Disposing of motorcycle waste

Many of the parts and fluids that your motorcycle uses are regarded as 'hazardous waste' when they come to the end of their usefulness. These parts and fluids include engine oil, brake fluid, transmission fluid, antifreeze fluid, oil filters, batteries and so on.

If you do your own bike servicing, make sure that you bring all your waste to a recycling centre or to a specialised hazardous waste recycling company licensed by the Environmental Protection Agency.

Disposing of bike maintenance waste in any other way is illegal and very damaging to the environment, and you could be prosecuted.

Disposing of your motorcycle

When a motorcycle comes to the end of its life, it must be disposed of in a controlled manner to ensure that it does not pose any threat to the environment.

There are authorised treatment facilities around the country that are licensed to perform this service without charge. Contact your local authority or a main dealer for your make of bike for further information. Owners of motorcycles that are disposed of illegally may face prosecution.

My commitment: 37

I understand the hazardous nature of motor waste and will never dispose of any waste except through licensed recycling centres.

Signed (Learner)

Dealing with collisions and emergencies

Arriving at the scene of a collision

If you are the first to arrive at the scene of a collision, there are a number of guidelines you need to follow:

- Stay calm, switch off your engine and assess the situation.
- Call the emergency services on 112 or 999. Don't assume that other people at the scene of the collision have already done that. Give the emergency services precise information about the nature of the collision, its location, and how many people you think are injured.
- Warn others about the collision – by turning on your hazard warning lights (if fitted) or by any other means you think necessary.
- Do not do anything to endanger your own safety. Make sure you are safe yourself before attending to other people. Place coats or rugs on anyone who is injured to keep them warm, but do not give them anything to eat or drink.
- Do not move an injured person, unless there is a real danger of fire or of a vehicle turning over. Do not remove helmets from injured motorcyclists. Do not try to lift a vehicle off an injured person without help.
- If you have time, draw a sketch or take photographs of the collision – these may be useful to the authorities investigating how the collision happened.

If you arrive at the scene of a collision and the emergency services are already there, ride on carefully and do not stop, unless you are asked to do so.

Reporting a collision

If you are involved in a collision in which anybody is injured, you must report it to An Garda Síochána, either to a garda at the scene or at a Garda station. If there is no garda at the scene, you must give your personal and vehicle details, including insurance details, to anyone involved in the collision and also to any independent witness who asks for this information.

My commitment: 38

If I am ever the first to arrive at the scene of a collision, I will respond quickly, calmly and responsibly, and will do nothing to further endanger the health or safety of anyone.

Signed (Learner)

Summary of commitments

My commitment: 1

I am willing to learn how to ride a motorcycle in a structured and controlled way with the help of a registered ADI. I will follow a course of Initial Basic Training.

Signed (Learner)

My commitment: 2

I will assess my own learning progress critically and honestly and will sign off on a topic only when I am confident I have mastered it fully.

Signed

My commitment: 3

I understand the responsibility of taking a motorcycle onto the road and of sharing the road with other people. I am ready to take on that personal responsibility and to take ownership of how I learn to ride a motorcycle..

Signed (Learner)

My commitment: 4

I understand the legal issues relating to riding a motorcycle and I commit myself to safe and responsible practice.

Signed (Learner)

My commitment: 5

I understand the importance of wearing a securely fastened safety helmet and appropriate protective clothing.

I will never ride a motorcycle without adequate protective clothing and a safety helmet.

I will maintain my protective clothing and helmet in good condition.

Signed (Learner)

My commitment: 6

I have studied all the motorcycle's controls and instruments. I know the purpose of each instrument and can operate each control.

Signed (Learner)

My commitment: 7

I know how to take the motorcycle on and off its stand, can mount and dismount easily, and can wheel the bike with the engine turned off.

Signed (Learner)

My commitment: 8

I have a good understanding of the basic service and maintenance requirements of my motorcycle and can carry out basic maintenance and checks myself.

Signed (Learner)

My commitment: 9

I am able to start the engine of the motorcycle, move off and stop safely in a traffic-free location.

Signed (Learner)

My commitment: 10

I am able to ride the motorcycle in a traffic-free location and can change gears.

Signed (Learner)

My commitment: 11

I understand the way that the front and rear brakes work, and I know how to use them in combination to slow down and stop.

Signed (Learner)

My commitment: 12

I am able to ride a motorcycle on the public road in a quiet location in very light traffic, with the support and advice of an ADI.

Signed (Learner)

My commitment: 13

I understand the importance of planning my practice journeys in advance and gaining experience of all kinds of road challenges.

Signed (Learner)

My commitment: 14

I am able to 'read the road' – to take in the information I need from changing traffic conditions, road markings, regulatory and warning signs, traffic lights, and direction signs.

Signed (Learner)

My commitment: 15

I know how to position my motorcycle on the road: I keep a safe distance between my motorcycle and the vehicle ahead; I understand how lanes work and can position my motorcycle in the appropriate lane at all times while on the road.

Signed (Learner)

My commitment: 16

I can safely negotiate all types of road junction – including left and right turns (from major to minor and from minor to major roads), slip roads, junctions with traffic lights, and roundabouts.

Signed (Learner)

My commitment: 17

I understand the importance of riding at speeds appropriate to the road conditions, and I will always ride within the legal speed limits.

Signed (Learner)

My commitment: 18

I know when and how to signal my intentions to other road users – including when to use direction indicators and the horn.

Signed (Learner)

My commitment: 19

I can usually interpret other road users' intentions – from the signals they give and also from subtle changes in their behaviour.

Signed (Learner)

My commitment: 20

I am able to overtake slower-moving vehicles.

However, I will do so only when it is necessary, legal and safe.

Signed (Learner)

My commitment: 21

I have practised advanced steering manoeuvres, and am confident that I have developed the control, balance and coordination necessary to control the motorcycle.

Signed (Learner)

My commitment: 22

I will always ride my motorcycle in a safe and responsible manner, and I will try to anticipate dangerous situations before they arise.

I have practised stopping very quickly as I may need to do this in a real emergency.

Signed (Learner)

My commitment: 23

I have a full motorcycle driving licence, have practised motorway riding and understand the challenges that it presents; and in particular, I appreciate the concentration required to ride for prolonged periods at high speed. I understand the importance of good route planning in advance of beginning a motorway journey.

Signed (Learner)

My commitment: 24

I have practised riding in heavy traffic. I am confident that I can control the motorcycle, remain patient, and deal with the frustrations of being stuck in traffic.

Signed (Learner)

My commitment: 25

I have practised riding my motorcycle at night on a variety of different roads, urban and rural. I understand the particular dangers of riding at night and will always ride with consideration for other road users.

Signed (Learner)

My commitment: 26

I have practised riding in conditions of poor daytime visibility. I appreciate the importance of seeing and being seen.

Signed (Learner)

My commitment: 27

I appreciate the dangers of riding a motorcycle in snow and ice, and I will not make any unnecessary journeys in such conditions.

When I do ride in snow and ice I will ride more slowly, leave more room ahead, and accelerate and brake smoothly and gently.

Signed (Learner)

My commitment: 28

I will always ride through road works with care and consideration; and I will obey the warning signs and any instructions the road workers give me.

Signed (Learner)

My commitment: 29

I have practised riding on urban streets and understand the particular hazards I am likely to come across there. I will always ride within the urban speed limit.

Signed (Learner)

My commitment: 30

I have practised riding on country roads and I understand that visibility might be poor and that the road surfaces might be more uneven than on urban or national roads.

While riding on country roads I will be considerate to the needs of farmers and other country dwellers and their animals.

Signed (Learner)

My commitment: 31

I accept that I am fully responsible for the safety and comfort of any pillion passenger I take with me on the road.

I will take a passenger only when I am satisfied that it is safe and legal to do so.

I understand that the motorcycle will handle differently with a passenger on board.

Signed (Learner)

My commitment: 32

I will ride a motorcycle only when I am physically and mentally fit to do so.

I will never ever drink and drive/ride.

I will never ever ride a motorcycle while under the influence of drugs (legal or illegal).

Signed (Learner)